P9-DCP-512

Renaissance
Exploration

Renaissance Exploration

J R Hale

 W · W · NORTON & COMPANY

New York · London

W. W. Norton & Company, Inc., 500 Fifth Avenue, New York, N.Y. 10110
W. W. Norton & Company Ltd., 37 Great Russell Street, London WC1B 3NU

COPYRIGHT © 1968 BY J. R. HALE

Library of Congress Catalog Card No. 73-170849

ISBN 393-00635-2

PRINTED IN THE UNITED STATES OF AMERICA

6 7 8 9 0

Contents

I

An Historical Perspective

This is a short book with a great theme: the sensationally rapid opening of the aperture through which Europeans looked at their world – the Cape of Good Hope rounded in 1488, the West Indies discovered in 1492, India reached by sea in 1498, Brazil described in 1500, the Americas recognized as a separate continent in 1513 by Balboa's sight of a new ocean, the Pacific. This was a climactic generation, possibly *the* climactic generation in world history, both for what was achieved and for the future significance of that achievement; but the pressure to explore, record and exploit was maintained, until by the end of the sixteenth century, with the exception of Australia and the Antarctic and of the northern coasts of America and Asia, the outlines of the world map were not drastically dissimilar to those in our own atlases.

The theme is not only vast in extent; it is sustained by a cast of characters, scores of whom deserve books to themselves. In few zones of action can 'Renaissance man' be observed so clearly as in the essentially individualistic, because independent and self-reliant, activity of exploration. To take only one and the most obvious example, Columbus; it is because of the freedom of action open to him, the lack of the fine mesh of communication and tradition that checked the personal volition of the Renaissance soldier or statesman or merchant, that the complexity of his nature emerges so strikingly. We see the mixture of clear-sightedness and wilful blindness, of practicality and superstition, of courageous endurance and deceit, with an added vividness because of the novelty and the isolation amidst which his decisions were made and his conclusions (stubbornly erroneous, some of them) reached. He and his companions were not, of course, free agents; they carried their preconceptions with them to Ternate or Labrador, they were, more or less vaguely, under orders, but through the explorers we can examine our Renaissance ancestors under, as it were, laboratory conditions. And it is by watching individuals encountering the unknown, and settlers coping with it, and intellectuals writing about it, that we can best discriminate between the engrained conditioning of medieval ideas and reactions, and the emergence of attitudes which seem to be new.

Indeed – and this is the justification for taking space for a preliminary discussion before reaching the events and the men themselves – to understand the phenomenon of world-wide exploration historically, we must first try to answer two questions: how far was it a natural development from the middle ages, and why, in a world of other advanced cultures – Mexican, Arab, Hindu – of cultures in some respects *more* sophisticated than that of Europe – Ming China, Higashiyama Japan – was it the Europeans who discovered them, and not *vice-versa*? For 'discovery' tends commonly to have too Eurocentric a ring instead of being used in the sense in which a Liverpudlian 'discovers' London on his first coach-trip south. It was there before he came, and his 'discovery' merely denotes his first personal contact with it. In the same way, the bedraggled European hitch-hikers who first penetrated India in the sixteenth century 'discovered' the thriving and fabulously wealthy state of Vijayanagar or found in the Emperor Babur a monarch who, for the brilliance of his conquests and the variety of his talents as administrator, poet and admirer of natural beauty, left his contemporary monarchs in Europe – Henry VIII, Francis I, Charles V – in the shade: he was nearer the ideal Renaissance man than any of them, although his court was Agra and his grave at Kabul. Our sense of the words 'explore' and 'discover' must include aspects such as these, as well as the purchase of vast tracts of jungle or prairie for a few handfuls of little bells. From the naked savages of Guiana to the silk-robed and contemptuous mandarins of Canton we are dealing with a process which is one of 'discovery' only if we look at it from the point of view of Europe. From a loftier vantage point it is the story not merely of an expanding continent but of civilizations previously isolated or uncertainly aware of one another being linked ever more closely by commercial and political entanglements, a world bound by a net of contacts; a world that, if we chose to be sentimental, seems, for its lack of secrets, to have become smaller.

How far, then, did expansion overseas develop naturally from the trading and political life of the middle ages? Columbus, Vasco da Gama and Magellan were the contemporaries of Leonardo da Vinci, Erasmus and Machiavelli. Because of this coincidence of dates, because the lifetime of Michelangelo (1475–1564) encompassed the greatest surge of exploration the world has ever known, it is tempting to see a necessary correspondence between the peak of Renaissance intellectual and artistic achievement on the one hand, and, on the other, the age of discovery. And this sense of mutual dependence is strengthened by one of the most potent formulations ever coined by a historian: Jules Michelet's summing up (1855) of the Renaissance as 'the discovery of the world and of man'. Could the discovery of the world have taken place without the discovery, by artists, poets and philosophers, of man – man, that is, as a self-confident, self-justifying individual to whose knowledge of self and questioning attitude to nature nothing is impossible?

The basic attitude of the explorer is a love of travel, a curiosity to see new lands, not out of need (as population pressures sent the Norsemen to Greenland) nor purely out of greed (as the Normans were attracted to Sicily) and not primarily for diversion (the motive that has produced much of the world's great travel literature, from Marco Polo to Doughty and Thesiger) but in the service of an organized vision of what might be found and an eagerness to relate it to what is known. Unlike the wanderer, who may however travel great distances and become an explorer unawares, the explorer sees himself as contributing to a sum of knowledge he has assessed beforehand.

From one point of view, life in late medieval Europe was static. Most men lived their lives within sight of the same hill or steeple, their baptisms and burials recorded in the same book. The outside world was something that came to them in the guise of a pedlar or friar, or a robber band or a tax-collector. But from another viewpoint, Europe was full of movement. Roads – where something that deserved to be called a road existed – were appalling; river transport was slow and expensive. Nevertheless, in spite of the hardships, the dangers and delays involved in travel, hundreds and thousands of men were constantly on the move. Masons, joiners and clock-makers were professional itinerants, so were the freelance soldiers who plied for hire between one trouble-spot and another. Scholars and students moved restlessly from one university to another, one patron to another, helped by the international passport of their Latinity. Painters and sculptors and architects travelled the length and breadth of Europe for their commissions: Spaniards worked in Italy, Italians in France, England, the Netherlands, Germany, Hungary and Russia. The great mosques of Constantinople were built by western architects, and other renegade Christians forged the cannon which the Turks used to conquer Egypt and to arm their fleets in the Mediterranean. Musicians, too, undertook long journeys from court to court, cathedral to cathedral, and there was even a class of pro-fessional tennis-players whom princes blithely bribed away from one another.

Besides what we might call the culture traffic, there was a constant flow of political traffic: ambassadors and lesser envoys, clerks and administrators, linking government with governed, estate with estate, lawyer with litigant. And scarcely less populous was the cleri-cal traffic between monasteries of the same order which stretched across Europe, between parish and cathedral and, from all parts of Christendom, to Rome. Busiest of all, of course, was the economic traffic, the merchants who travelled the great trunk trade routes, attended the international and national fairs and threaded with a single cart or mule into the tiny distribution centres of the remotest countryside.

To those who wanted or needed to travel, then, travel was pos-sible, and we have seen how numerous they were. And when we add the thriving sea routes, the regular plying of Venetian galleys to England, of Baltic traders to Spain, we get a picture of a Europe tense with movement, a ceaseless traffic swelling in volume as the population of consumers recovered from the Black Death and its wake of lesser pestilences. On the eve of the great discoveries the commercial machinery of Europe was purposeful and sophisticated; a far-flung oceanic trade was there in embryo. There were ships for all purposes; fast galleys for a speedy traffic in luxuries, wallowing broad-beamed merchantmen for the long haul of bulk goods: wine, skins, wool and grain; nimble lateeners that could nose accurately up creeks and estuaries; fishing craft able to stand up to weeks of gales on the high seas as the catch was salted and stored. Credit facilities and insurance were available for long voyages on which the return might be slow or chancy. Around the towering merchant and banking firms like the Medici and Fugger with their widely scattered branches and agencies were a multitude of smaller concerns. And though historians still argue about the meaning of capitalism in the fifteenth century, and though the church preached, and governments tried to enforce, the doctrine of the non-usurious just price, the preoccupation with how to make a profit was universal, from the papal bankers to those small-town congregations who were so often scolded from the pulpit for chattering about buying and selling and contracts during divine service.

Nor was Europe a totally closed community. Spices from the East Indies, silks and drugs and ceramics from China came to the pick-up ports of Egypt and Syria by way of junks to India, dhows to the Red Sea and camels to the Mediterranean, or via the long overland routes to the ports of the Black Sea, picking up further luxuries in Persia on the way. In the ports of North Africa could be bought gold from beyond the Sahara and the spice known as grains of paradise which was used as a pepper-substitute. On the midfifteenth century quaysides of Venice and Southampton goods could be bought which had come from Benin and Borneo. And an appetite for the products of the world beyond Europe was growing. Precious metals were in short supply. They were needed as a medium of exchange and as a reserve, and the demand was the greater for the growing reluctance of governments to allow the circulation of coin beyond national frontiers. It was in part this policy that led, especially in fifteenth century France, to the encouragement of native industries to counter the drain of gold and silver abroad, and the tonic effect of this enterprise involved still more transactions requiring coin. Increased production in the silver mines, especially those of Germany, was a temporary palliative, but there was an acute gold-hunger throughout Europe, of which one symptom (and exacerbation) was the taking of coin out of circulation by hoarding.

Another product in mounting demand was spices, especially cinnamon, cloves, nutmeg and pepper. They were used in medicines and to disguise the flavour of bad, as well as to enhance the savour of good, food. Hardly a necessity, by the fifteenth century the use of spices had become something in the nature of an addiction, and the demand, and the price paid, made cloves and pepper the equivalents of the tea, tobacco and coffee of the future.

With vessels of many types and experienced long-passage mariners, with an energetic body of merchants, some of whom by the values of today would be millionaires, gold-hungry and spice-addicted Europe could afford to feel that if supplies dwindled and it were necessary to fight a way to their source 'we've got the ships, we've got the men, we've got the money too'. And the jingoism, as we shall see, was provided by a crusading yet pragmatic Christianity.

The challenge of dwindling supplies – and it is possible that even a static rate of supply would have been challenge enough – came in the fifteenth century. The supply of trans-Saharan gold was uncertain, at the mercy of profiteering Arab middlemen and, still more, of tribal wars in the interior. The road-block pushed by the Turks across Asia Minor intercepted the land spice route, and Turkish galleys in the eastern Mediterranean harassed the outlet from Alexandria. There were trade agreements with the Christian trading states, especially with Venice, and there was smuggling, but the volume of goods became uncertain, and, what with Turkish tolls and enhanced insurance rates, the trade became more expensive. Throughout the century men thought of outflanking the entrepôts and going to the source.

Here lay the rub. How did you get there? Land routes were out of the question. Europeans had crossed the Sahara, but the trade was firmly in native and Arab hands, and even if Europeans could take over the caravans the price of gold and paradise grains would be much the same on reaching the Sahara, indeed more, because of the cost involved in taking over the routes and protecting them. Europeans, among whom Marco Polo was only one, had travelled overland in Asia during the period between the mid-thirteenth and mid-fourteenth century when, for political reasons, travel was reasonably safe through Persia and the colossal Mongol empire. In 1245, Giovanni de Plano Carpini and in 1253 William de Rubruquis travelled to Karakorum near Lake Baikal. In 1256, or thereabouts, Niccolo and Maffeo Polo left Constantinople for China and spent fourteen years in Peking at the court of Kublai Khan. Still more expressive of the possibilities of long-distance travel when the hazards were only those of hardship and nature, the brothers returned to Venice, only to set out once more for China with Niccolo's son Marco, aged fifteen. They went via Arabia (a false start, aiming to take shipping at Ormuz in the Persian Gulf), Persia, the wild plateau of the Pamirs, which lies at the northern junction of the Pakistan-Indian frontier, Tibet and the Gobi desert. After a second stay, this time of seventeen years, the return was made by sea via the Malay Peninsula, Sumatra, South India and the south Persian coast and thence overland by the spice route Tabriz, Trebizond, Constantinople, Venice. As a result of these journeys, and others that followed, it was clear that the route to China, where the spices of the Moluccas could be bought subject only to the freight charges for the Celebes and South China Seas, was a practicable one. But, again, even if it were politically safe, it took thirty-five times as much energy to transport goods by land as by sea, and the overland freight charges, as goods were changed from pony- to horse- to camel-caravans, would be as heavy as if the European merchant had waited for his goods to be delivered in Aleppo or Constantinople. And there was not much advantage either in sitting on one's bales as they were changed from craft to craft from Indonesia across the Indian Ocean before facing the handling charges and customs dues of Suez and Alexandria. This astonishing century of Asian travel showed that in conditions of political security a European could hop from route to route, animal to animal, craft to craft and go wherever he wanted – but it showed too, that it was not worth it. Even in the fifteenth century Europeans got to the Far East; Niccoló Conti, for instance, another

Venetian, began in 1419 a journey that was to take him via Baghdad and Ormuz to Goa, Sumatra and Java. But such a journey – and there were successors, culminating in the marvellous narrative published by Ludovico Varthema in 1510 – was irrelevant to the merchant; it involved dyeing one's face, learning Arabic, not being shown up as a non-Moslem on pilgrim caravans, waiting months at a time for onward transport or relying on one's legs, marrying locally (as Conti married an Indian girl) or pretending to be mad (as Varthema did to get released from gaol). To the obsessive wanderer, these were obstacles to take in one's stride, even (in retrospect, at least) to welcome, but to the merchants they damned the overland route as impractical. He would have to go by sea.

At this point we enter our story proper. No ship had ever come from the East to Europe, no European ship had ever been to Cathay – and Cathay, far more than the Gulf of Guinea (from whose northern littoral came the trans-Saharan gold) was looked on as *the* source; Marco Polo's narrative, multiplied and re-multiplied in manuscript, had given (erroneously) the impression that Cathay was a fabulously rich source of gold as well as spices. So there was a technical problem: the blazing of a trail by sea, and this could only be done by exploring the route. But there was also an imaginative problem: what was the route likely to be?

In the fifteenth century there were three types of map which men could use to imagine what the world looked like. One was the Jerusalem map, or *mappamundi*. This was not a map for use, not an aid to imagining what the world really looked like. From Jerusalem at the centre (such maps were commonly round) the rest of creation – Europe, Africa and Asia that is – was crammed in as a commemoration of the divine purpose in creating sea and land. It was a visual equivalent of Genesis, an aid to meditation spiced with the names of places famous for size or sanctity or legend. Its purpose was above all Christian, not practical. It was irrelevant to the explorer.

A second type was the Ptolomaic map, derived from the *Geographia* of the second century A.D. cartographer, Claudius Ptolemy of Alexandria. The Ptolomaic world map showed the world as it had been known in that era: a world that, thanks to Greek contact with India and guesses derived from rumour and trade about what lay beyond, gave a more or less accurate lay-out of Europe, the North African coastline and Arabia, and allotted generous space to the Indian Ocean – showing it, however, as an inland sea, with its southern shore washing the vast (and entirely speculative) mass of Terra Incognita, which was shown north of and parallel to the Tropic of Capricorn, and blending at that point into Africa.

Unlike the mainly symbolic Jerusalem maps, the Ptolemy maps frequently had north (instead of east) at the top, and were oval or rectangular, with their right halves given up to Asia, thus providing room for information derived from medieval accounts of the Far East, like that of Marco Polo. In spite of their inaccuracies, especially with regard to India, Ceylon, the Malay Peninsula and the East Indies, they were at least an attempt to give a visual picture of what the world looked like, and encouragingly showed that, once in the Indian Ocean, a vessel could sail straight to the Spice Islands and Cathay.

The Ptolemaic tradition of classical cartography was, then, paradoxical. It provided a map of the right shape, on which information of the right sort could be inserted, and it showed the sea-route that was needed stretching clear from East Africa to the land of cloves and gold. But it also seemed to show that there was no way of breaking into that route: it gave a teasingly clear view of the treasure and, at the same time, locked the door on it.

The text of the *Geographia*, too, took back with one hand what it gave with the other. On the credit side was Ptolemy's assertion that life was possible, that there were men living in the Southern Hemisphere. If this were so, then they must have moved down below the equator from the north, for the medieval church taught that all men were descended from the sons of Noah. And this implied that were ships to test the truth of Ptolemy's assumption that it was impossible to circumnavigate Africa, their crews at least would not be scorched to death while trying to cross the equator. The strength of this last belief can be seen from the account given of a story picked up in Portugal by a Bohemian traveller in 1466.

'Once a king of Portugal sent out two ships and two galleys from this place to see what lay beyond and whether there was any land there. The ships were provisioned for several years and were away three years, but only one galley returned and even on that galley most of the crew had died. And those which survived could hardly be recognized as human. They had lost flesh and hair, the nails had gone from hands and feet. Their eyes were sunk deep in their heads and they were as black as Moors. They spoke of the incredible heat which was such that it was a marvel that ships and crews were not burnt. They said also that they found no houses or land and they could sail no farther. The farther they sailed, so the sea became more furious and the heat grew more intense. They thought that the other ships had sailed too far and it was impossible that they should be able to return.'

But while Ptolemy – and we must remember that in the fifteenth century classical authors were acquiring the sort of authority hitherto accorded only to Holy Writ and the Fathers of the Church – encouraged exploration on this point, on another, and crucial, point he was unhelpful. All persons concerned with trade or navigation in the late middle ages believed that the world was round – anyone searching for landmarks at sea is aware of the earth's curvature. It followed, then, that if you sailed off one side of a Ptolemy map you would reappear on the opposite side. The point had been made clearly by Strabo, another classical writer on geography (a predecessor of Ptolemy) who was studied carefully in fifteenth century humanist circles. 'The inhabited world', he had written, 'forms a complete circle, itself meeting itself. So that if the immensity of the Atlantic Sea did not prevent, we could sail from Iberia [Spain] to India along one and the same parallel over the remainder of the circle.' And the idea was stated clearly again by the Florentine mathematician and cosmographer Paolo da Pozzo Toscanelli, who was consulted about routes to Cathay in 1474 by King Alfonso of Portugal; he wrote to a Portuguese correspondent in that year saying, of the spice source in the East, 'these regions can be reached by sailing due West'.

On most maps of the period, however, Europe was crammed against one margin and Asia against the other, and no map showed an Atlantic of anything like its real extent, with the possible exception of the Vinland Map (c. 1440), whose authenticity is still open to some doubt. It was, however, assumed that an ocean reached far further westwards than Atlantic fishing vessels normally went and there was a lively crop of legends about islands to be found there: Atlantis, St Brandon's Isle, the Land of Fair Women, the Isle of Weepers, and others equally legendary. What was less certain was whether the Ocean Sea, as it was commonly called, was capable of supporting life; it was the possibility that the Ocean Sea was a fatal area, not the possibility of falling over the world's edge, that led to a fear of running 'off the map'. Ptolemy gave no guidance on this point, but Strabo implied that life was possible anywhere on the globe and thus encouraged those – like Columbus – who thought of reaching Cathay by heading west. And Strabo gave encouragement to the idea that Africa could be circumnavigated, an idea also put forward in the work of Caius Julius Solinus, another classical author, whose work was largely concerned with marvels and monsters but was all the more popular in the middle ages on that account.

A fascinating summary of geographical knowledge and theory in the mid-fifteenth century is provided in a famous world map (1459) by the Venetian monk Fra Mauro. This large work – it is over six feet in diameter – is round like the Jerusalem Maps associated with monastic scriptoria, but it gives an almost Ptolemaic space to Asia – and adapts Ptolemaic outlines for it – and it shows an Africa which, while weird in shape and not taking even reasonably full account of Portuguese discoveries by that date (possibly as far south as Sierra Leone), is clearly circumnavigable. Here at last was a view of the world which put the spice-and-gold details of medieval travellers to the Far East in a Ptolemaic – i.e. 'realistic' – framework and unlocked the door which Ptolemy himself had closed by running Africa into Terra Incognita.

Fra Mauro's map also draws to some extent on the techniques of the third type of map, the portolan. The portolan was, unlike the Jerusalem or Ptolemaic maps, designed not for pious contemplation or scholarly reference but for use. On land the traveller relied on knowing an itinerary and asking the way – he needed little more than a strip of names. But at sea, where there was no one to ask, the mariner needed to know how to find his way from landfall to landfall by plotting a course in terms of compass bearings and wind direction. These landfalls – harbours, capes and inlets – had to be accurately spaced or the compass bearings between them would not work out, and as a result by the fifteenth century the portolans gave a highly accurate picture of the coasts of northern Europe and the Mediterranean, and their techniques were applied, as soon as rough surveys could be completed, to newly discovered lands.

The pilot on an ordinary trading voyage in familiar waters needed only the map-type which had evolved from medieval needs: the portolan. But the portolan, being essentially a record of what was known, was no use to a voyager facing the unknown; he needed an indication of what he would find beyond portolan range and it is here that the humanist study of cartography – speculation in terms of modified Ptolomaic world maps – supplemented the medieval sea chart with Renaissance theory and made exploration (planned discovery) possible. The theories were often erroneous; sometimes, as in the case of the theoretical north-west and north-east passages, they led to scores of deaths in searches for the impossible; sometimes a theory postulated a continent that was not there – Terra Australis; all were ignorant of a continent that was there – the Americas; but without a theory mariners like Columbus and Magellan would not have sailed, could not have found backers. This is the chief point, perhaps it is the only point, where an aspect of the intellectual Renaissance intervened to help a process that was leading naturally from medieval international trade to interoceanic commerce.

And it is tempting to see here the influence of the treatment of space in Renaissance art. In the middle ages there were two ways of 'seeing' space; unrealistic in art, realistic for men moving about their fields or going to market. Influenced by the purely conventional treatment of space in art it may well have been, though it cannot be proved, that when men thought about distances beyond their immediate knowledge they thought in these conventional terms and 'saw' remote distances in the unrealistic terms of art. It may have been this fact that accounted for the long survival of the Jerusalem maps and, indeed, there are traces of this double standard in the reluctance of cartographers to amend even the Ptolomaic maps in response to the new information that flooded in after the great voyages. Some of the more decorative portolans show this double

18

standard very clearly: realistic coastlines – the area the mariner knew and used, and pictures in the interior – the area beyond his need for knowledge – of scenes and groups painted in the unrealistic conventions of medieval art. Indeed, one could generalize by saying that in almost all medieval maps the urge to record space realistically fades beyond the limits of the known world and cartographers are content to repeat traditional patterns, crowd in the place-names and legends of medieval travel literature according to the principles of a catalogue rather than of a visually realized itinerary, and bend their coastlines to fit the map's format rather than *vice-versa*. To the dangers and uncertainties of long-range exploration was added a difficulty in imagining the goal in real spatial terms.

During the fifteenth century, however, the double standard was challenged by a widely-shared (and still incompletely explained) determination among artists to record space realistically. It is the century of perspective, of the rationally organized landscape, a century in which the study of mathematics, and especially of geometry, so important both to navigation and cartography, becomes a passion. And it is perhaps not straining the evidence too far to suggest that this realistic way of thinking about and recording space made it easier to 'see' the whole world as open to investigation.

However, though a specifically 'Renaissance' atmosphere surrounds the origins of some of the great late-fifteenth and early-sixteenth century voyages of discovery (a fruitful liaison between scholar-cosmographers, learned mariners, enlightened rulers and educated backers) there had been a trial-run for the great discoveries in a purely medieval setting. In the fourteenth century the Atlantic island groups, the Azores, the Madeiras and the Canaries provided a nursery of experience for the longer African and Atlantic voyages. All these groups were discovered in the fourteenth century, mainly by Genoese sailing from Portugal. The Canaries were already on a sea chart in 1389, the Madeiras appeared on a map in 1351, and the same map, in the so-called 'Medici Atlas' in the Laurenciana Library in Florence, shows the Azores, both groups being portrayed with portolan-like accuracy. Moreover, voyages to and from the islands were made with some regularity. Nine separate expeditions to the Canaries alone have been traced between 1336 and 1393, and this can only represent a fraction of the voyages actually made. The Azores – which were used as a staging post by Columbus and his successors – are a third of the way across the Atlantic, and though they and the other island groups can be reached by sailing down-wind, the winds and currents made the journey a matter of fairly sophisticated compass navigation over great distances of open water; it has been suggested that the experience of these voyages lay behind the efforts of Prince Henry the Navigator of Portugal to sponsor what we would call research into navigational techniques with the exploration of the African coast south of the Canaries in view, especially with regard to the transference of position-finding by means of the sun and stars from use on land to practice at sea.

An account of African coastal exploration in the early fifteenth century belongs to the next chapter. The point I wish to make here is that the Atlantic triangle Lisbon – Azores – Cape Bojador (mapped on the Catalan Atlas of 1375) provided a training school for ships and seamen, competent, in all but vision, for exploration at any range. The fifteenth and sixteenth centuries were to see some improvements in navigational techniques, in compass and instrument design and the improvement of the astronomical tables on which their use depended, but the use of these improved position-finding techniques was not fundamental to navigation or map-making, indeed they led on occasion to grotesque miscalculations. Nor did improved ship design, handier sail plans and trimmer hulls alter the fact that given a firmly imagined goal for westward exploration the seamen of the fourteenth century could have discovered America and returned to tell the tale.

These early Atlantic sailings were made with few and small ships and, as far as we can tell, with individual rather than state support. And this pattern continued into the High Renaissance. From at least 1480 Bristol merchants sent out ships singly or in pairs to prospect across the Atlantic (the Iceland trade lay behind this, and the knowledge of Greenland, whither Christian I of Denmark sent an expedition in 1473 to resume the lapsed contact between Greenland and Scandinavia). John Cabot reached Newfoundland in 1497 in a single ship of fifty tons and a crew of eighteen or twenty men. The Portuguese exploration of the African coast south of Cape Bojador was carried out in the main by single ships. Columbus himself left on his first voyage with three ships and a total crew of ninety. Magellan, setting off for what was intended to be a round-the-world voyage, was given five ships mustering a total tonnage of four hundred and seventy tons between them. And this at a time when ships of over a thousand tons were not rare. The pattern remains the same throughout the period of the great discoveries: one, two or three ships are the rule and small, inexpensive, and often old and battered ones.

The capital involved did not, therefore, require the riches we associate with the cultivated courts and international financiers of the Renaissance. The ships employed were not the vessels built in arsenals, like the rigidly controlled galleys of Venice, or in royal dockyards with a degree of supervision – and additional expense – suitable to ships of special purpose like warships and 'prestige' giant merchantmen. They were built in small local yards not expressly for discovery but for the rough and tumble of general purpose trade, and their voyages were often paid for by local shipbuilders and merchants – Columbus' *Pinta*, from the small ship-building port of Palos, was the property of her crew. Moreover, the cargo they took with them, to Africa and across the Atlantic, was cheap: nails, little mirrors and bells, combs – geegaws to barter with for gold. When it came to following up the discoveries, to exploiting new trade-routes, establishing colonies and organizing convoys, then the great international figures of Renaissance commerce were called in to provide capital and share risks, but the history of Renaissance exploration, from the financial point of view, involved no more money than could be mustered by a thousand medieval merchants of moderate prosperity. The influence of the Fuggers and the Welsers was there, but its role was to greet the successful explorer with the golden applause of their investment in later voyages of exploitation.

We have gone some way towards answering our first question: how far was Renaissance exploration a natural development from the middle ages? And we have seen that in nearly all respects, excepting the role of geographical theory, it was. The motives – trade, especially the search for gold and spices; the means – ships, maps, the essential navigational knowledge; the men: there was nothing essentially new there. And if we add another motive, crusading zeal, the desire to convert the infidel or the irreligious savage, this is in a tradition that goes back to the crusades and it was, besides, usually mingled with other motives – also old ones: greed, adventure, curiosity. Though the protestations of princes might for form's sake (and not necessarily insincerely) put religion first, it is wiser to use the formula attributed to Vasco da Gama who sailed to India in search of both 'spices and Christians'.

The second question was: why in a world of many civilizations was it the Europeans who took the initiative in discovery?, and, by extension, how were they able to get away with it, to come and go, to swagger across the globe, as if they possessed some mysterious immunity? This, too, must be answered in any attempt to put the exploration movement into the perspective of world history.

The first condition for exploration was the possession of adequate ships. These were possessed only by Europeans. During the fifteenth century remarkable voyages were being made in the Southern Indian Ocean and in the Pacific by large outrigger sailing canoes, but these, while suited to crossing between Madagascar and the mainland, or from one Pacific island to another, were dependent on favourable following winds and known currents; they could not fight into the wind as an explorer's craft had to do. Similarly junks were regularly making the long passage from Canton round the Malay Peninsula to ports like Cochin and Malabar on the west coast of India. But the junk, though an admirable cargo carrier, was also dependent on following winds. Its flat bottom gave it a pronounced side-slip when the wind moved abeam, and its sweep-like rudder was vulnerable in high seas. Using the monsoons, the junk could sail immense distances, but, like the outrigger, it was not nimble or hardy enought for exploration which required ships that could sail fairly close up to the wind and hold their own in a storm without fleeing helplessly before it. The explorer needed a tough ship that he could aim (as nearly was possible in the days of sail) in the direction he wanted to go. Similarly, though the Indian Ocean was criss-crossed with dhows trading between India, the Red Sea and East Africa, these Arab vessels, their planking sewn with coconut fibre rope and rigged for the triangular lateen sail which is still a familiar sight in the east, were not suited to exploration. Sewn planking is weaker on the open sea than nailed, and the huge lateen boom requires a larger crew than is needed on a ship provided with a number of square sails, a crucial point when voyages of uncertain duration were embarked upon.

It is true, of course, that almost anything that will float and which has some sort of a sail can travel immense distances. Thor Heyerdahl, for instance, has made a persuasive case for the settlement of Polynesia by rafts like his own *Kon Tiki* sailing across the Pacific from South America. The Norsemen crossed the Atlantic in the tenth century to Greenland and thence to the St. Lawrence in open boats, probably with a single sail. But there we are dealing with peoples desperately short of space at home and prepared to take almost any risks to improve their standard of living by migrating elsewhere. Explorers are as anxious to get back to their own countries as they are to leave them. No European country was direly over-populated during the Renaissance. The chief motive behind the voyages was profit, not settlement, and there was no point in finding a new market or source of wealth if news of it could not be brought home.

It was during the late middle ages, and in European waters, that ships were developed that could go anywhere and get back. Behind this development is a peculiarly European situation, the existence of two distinct ship-building traditions: the stout, broad, square-sailed trader of the North Sea and the Atlantic coast, and the long-oared galley and the lateen-rigged coaster of the Mediterranean. Increasing trade between these two areas led to a mingling of types, drawing on the best features of ships evolved to sail in an inland sea and the open ocean. The result was the go-anywhere, do-anything craft of the explorers. And there was a further advantage possessed only by European ships, guns firing not only fore and aft but broadside through ports cut in the ship's high sides. This not only meant that European naval gunnery was uniquely effective but that fighting tactics did not rely on the large crew needed (as in the case of the junk) to row fast enought to ram or to grapple and board. The European ship fought best by holding off and using its cannon, and it did not have to see its stores consumed by soldiers; the seamen could fight the ship as well as sail it.

It may seem unromantic to deal in these terms. But what we are concerned with is not the *wanderlust* that has, in all ages, sent individuals on long and perilous journeys, but with a period in which governments increasingly harnessed and fostered and exploited this instinct in the service of material gain. So we must not only be interested in individual explorers, but in the psychological and social forces that called them into being and gave them their chance.

Psychologically, what distinguished Europeans as a whole from other races at this time, was an activist individualism. In spite of kings, feudal customs, priests and guilds, the individual's liberty was less circumscribed than in caste-divided India or family-centred China or under the priest-kings of Central and Southern America. In spite of plagues and local famines, moreover, the standard of living in Europe was higher than elsewhere; Europe was sufficiently comfortably off to want to become rich. Again, Europe was not like China, with a government strong at the centre and weak at the extremities, it was a densely packed mosaic of thriving, thrusting, independent states, jealous of one another, determined not to be left behind in any race for prestige or possible power. In this respect, the Sea Race was not unlike the Space Race.

In Christianity, moreover, Europeans had a religion as militant and expansionist as that of Islam, and one that in practice allowed as much scope for profit as for prophets. However much historians anguish over the theoretical split between the teaching of both the Catholic and the Protestant churches on the question of profit (which both thought should be minimal) on the one hand, and the soaring interest rates encouraged by the business community on the other, if we look at the story of exploration there is no conflict at all. Here, for instance, in a letter to be handed over to any potentates an English expedition might come across in their search for a (mythical) passage to China round northern Europe, is Edward VI's opinion of God's endorsement of the merchant's way of life. 'For the God of heaven and earth, greatly providing for mankind, would not that all things should be found in one region, to the end that one should have need of another that by this means friendship might be established among all men and every one seek to gratify all.' No great endeavour, moreover, however materialistic its real aim, can be sustained without the fuel of idealism. Capital, colony, nation: these words were powered into great historical forces by the philosophy which placed an 'ism' at their tail. Exploration, planned by canny merchants and acquisitive kings, relied on a redirection of the Christian crusading impulse as one of its recruiting officers and its most publicized justification.

An advanced technology, a dynamic morale: these factors lay behind this great phase of European expansion. Suitable ships, competitive nations, an economy flexible enough to let an adventurous country draw on the resources of inland stay-at-home ones as Spain drew on German bankers, missionary zeal: all these added up to a thrust that nowhere encountered an equally powerful technological ability, or a comparable will to resist.

Easiest of all races for Europeans to dominate were the really primitive races like the Arawaks of the West Indies and the Tupinamba of Brazil. Still at the Neolithic stage of migrant agriculture, docile and with no power of original thought or co-ordinated self-protection, they were easy victims: the Arawaks were almost entirely wiped out by Columbus' successors. The Indians who lived in North America between the Carolinas and the Great Lakes, Cherokees, Hurons, Iroquois, were hunters and a higher degree of political organization enabled them to put up a fierce resistance. But the way they thought made it impossible for them to learn from their enemies. For them there was no such thing as an abstract idea; animals, plants, stones, weapons were all connected with the world of spirits. Their perception was based on a confused acceptance of a world filled with magical objects; they had not reached that stage of culture when men evaluate, criticize, experiment and create. Unlike the Arawaks, they could not be exterminated, but they could be held back from areas which Europeans wished to occupy.

Much further advanced were the Mayas of Mexico, who had a stable agriculture, cities and a loosely federated political organization. They were literate, used numbers, including zero (a concept far beyond the range of any North American race), and a systematized

25

hierarchy of gods. It was fortunate for Cortes that their weapons were more primitive than their thought processes and that on his arrival they were weakened by civil wars.

It was one of the ironies of history that the most advanced peoples of the Americas, the Aztecs of central Mexico and the Incas of Peru were more vulnerable to the Spaniards than most of the primitive ones. Against savages like the Chichimecs the Spaniards could do no more than they could against untameable animals. But after defeat in battle the intricate administrative systems of the Aztecs and Incas could be taken over entirely, and the people, used to order and obedience, resigned themselves to serving their new masters. It was, again, fortunate for the Spaniards that these nations too were gravely weakened by political jealousies, but even here victory was partly due to the undeflecting will to win of the Spaniards which pierced the basic fatalism in their opponents' characters as surely as their guns pierced their armour.

It is remarkable that Christianity, for all its monasteries and mystics, was of all the creeds existing in the world of Columbus' day the one most suited to men of action. Its nearest rival was Islam, the cutting edge of whose expansion – Constantinople fell in 1453, Vienna was besieged in 1529 – was the individual's belief that death in a battle against infidels meant an eternity of haremic bliss; such a death was proof of faith and would be suitably rewarded. The Christian believed the former part of this credo but was more canny about the latter. Christian morality emphasized the good life more than the worthy death, and to the ordinary man the Christian heaven lacked the concrete appeal of the worldly pleasures promised by the Moslem paradise; the Christian valued courage plus survival above a fanatical self-immolation. This crusading streak in Mohammedanism was accompanied by a tolerance, after conquest, of other faiths that was beyond anything Christians could feel during the Renaissance or, indeed, for long after. Europeans believed that the way they thought and lived was altogether superior to the habits of other peoples and at the same time they were conscious, as men of other faiths were not, of a double desire: to live both morally and physically better lives. While the Moslem, and still more the Buddhist and the Hindu, took his environment for granted, believing the world and the business of making a living in it to be of secondary importance to the world of the spirit, the Christian believed that God had made the world for him to make the best of: he saw it as something to be enjoyed rather than endured.

This is putting the contrast too simply, of course, and leaving out differences of race, climate and political and economic organization. But there was a difference of temperament and will between explorers and explored and it is better to seize it with blunt tools than with none.

Indeed, the most aggressive Moslem power, the Ottoman Turks, realized this themselves. They trained captured Christian boys to rise to the highest offices in the administration and in the army. Skilled renegades, especially engineers, were always welcome. It was thanks to renegade Christians that the Turks had a siege artillery powerful enough to pound breaches in the walls of Constantinople. But their artillery in other respects soon fell behind that of Europe: their field guns and their use of guns at sea were never a challenge to the voyagers or to the little armies they left behind them in areas like the Persian Gulf, the East African coast or Moslem India.

Further east it was the same story. The Chinese of the Ming period belonged to an Empire whose intellectual and artistic achievements were even more refined than those of Europe. They believed their civilization to be the finest in the world and looked on all foreigners as barbarians. But partly for religious reasons, partly because of the inertia that beset a vast, intricate and increasingly corrupt bureaucracy, they showed as a nation an almost senile complacence in contrast to the brash peoples of Europe whose aggressiveness, whose eagerness for technological progress and whose loud confidence appalled them. A Renaissance European was regarded in China rather as a buoyant Yankee was shuddered from in the more exquisite drawing-rooms of nineteenth-century Europe.

Moreover, when Europeans began to explore the world in the fifteenth century China had given up conquest, even contact with other nations and withdrawn inside its own borders. Immensely conservative, seeing no point in fresh ideas, profoundly respectful of traditional learning, seeing the family as far more important than the individual, the Chinese were able to baffle and exclude Europeans without ever wanting to compete with them for markets like the Philippines and the Moluccas which were at their very doors.

The position in Japan was not dissimilar. Again we have a culture of exceptional brilliance. The painting of the Muromachi period is comparable in vigour, sureness and variety with that of Europe. The architecture, not only of temples but of delicately elaborate pleasure buildings like the Golden and Silver Pavilions of Kyoto and of villas like Ryôanji – more harmoniously rational living spaces than Europe built before the twentieth century – coincides with the Age of Discovery. But in Japan as in China technology and science was despised, and the country, barely kept from anarchy by the Ashikaga shoguns, remained economically primitive. And when peace was restored, when the country – had it temperamentally wished – could have looked out into the world as it did so dramatically in the nineteenth century, the decision was taken to imitate the narcissism of China. In 1636 the shogun Iyemitsu forbade any Japanese to leave the country – or to return to it from any contaminating residence abroad – on pain of death.

Alone of civilized peoples, then, Europeans had the technical and psychological equipment, and the political and economic background, to carry out a sustained programme of exploration. And wherever they went they found peoples either too primitive or too ill-armed, too confused by local rivalries or too indifferent to the 'unreal' here and preoccupied with the 'real' hereafter, to oppose them. There were failures, a landfall that could not be made, a settlement – like the Roanoke colony – wiped out, but most commonly these were the result of tempest or malnutrition, or of rivals from Europe itself. What Europeans decided to do they could do; only the forces of nature, it seemed, could stop them. It was a lesson that bolstered their pride – and has bedevilled attempts at interracial co-operation ever since.

2
Africa and the East

Three generations of African exploration preceded Columbus' discovery of America, and, at least from the 1480s, when a conviction was growing that the continent could be circumnavigated, Africa itself was increasingly seen as secondary in importance to the eventual exploitation of the East. It is convenient, then, to treat the exploration of Africa, India and the Far East as a whole.

It is customary to date the exploration of Africa from 1419, when Prince Henry the Navigator was made governor of the Algarve and established an observatory at Sagres, in the south-west corner of Portugal. Here he drew together, in a manner we can only fitfully catch sight of, astronomers, geographers and mathematicians. From here he sent out expeditions which had got as far as Cape Bojador – with a glimpse beyond – by 1434. Though the records are scanty, it is clear that Henry's fame is justified as the first rational organizer of exploration as an expanding reconnaissance based on co-operation between pilots at sea and experts at headquarters. While not dissimilar to the methods by which the Venetians had slowly extended their Levantine and Atlantic-North Sea trade routes, this is the first example of a programme of discovery being put into effect.

This first phase was cautious, and its purpose was probably to verify what was already guessed. Uncertain attempts to sketch the West African coast as far as the Gulf of Guinea had already appeared on certain fourteenth century maps, and these may have recorded information that reached North Africa from the Saharan caravans and from the coastal trade between West African settlements and the

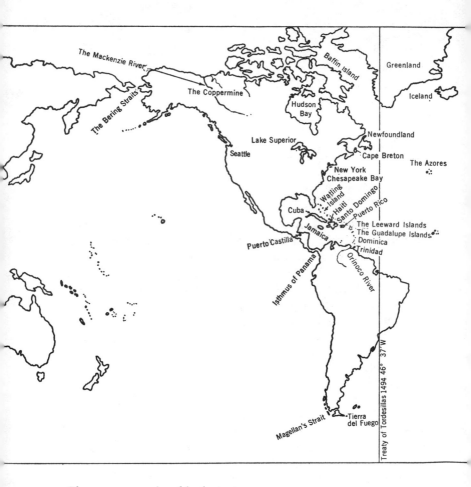

Place-names mentioned in the text.

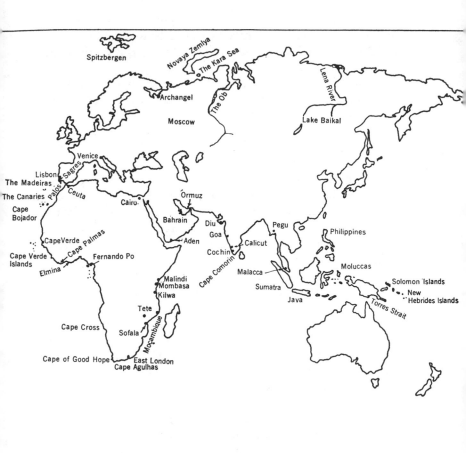

Spitzbergen

Novaya Zemlya

The Kara Sea

Archangel

The Ob

Lena River

Moscow

Lake Baikal

Venice

Lisbon

Sagres

The Madeiras

Palos

The Canaries

Ceuta

Ôrmuz

Cape Bojador

Cairo

Bahrain

Diu

Goa

Pegu

Philippines

CapeVerde

Cape Palmas

Aden

Calicut

Cape Verde Islands

Fernando Po

Cochin

Cape Comorin

Malacca

Moluccas

Elmina

Malindi

Mombasa

Sumatra

Solomon Islands

Kilwa

Java

New

Hebrides Islands

Torres Strait

Tete

Cape Cross

Sofala

Moçambique

Cape of Good Hope

East London

Cape Agulhas

big Moorish ports near the Atlantic end of the Mediterranean, ports like Ceuta, which Henry himself captured and where he spent some time in 1415. Nor is it out of the question that in Lisbon useful information could be picked up from the thousands of Moorish slaves in the city. Be that as it may, it still required unusual vision on Henry's part, and unusual boldness from his captains, for not only was there danger from natives – the first Portuguese known to have landed were attacked – but there were mythical terrors both by sea (the boiling equator) and land.

The folk-lore about Africa and Asia was rich and widely known. The Greeks had known India, the Romans had patrolled and settled parts of Asia Minor and Africa. Their historians had written of these areas, and listened attentively to the stories filtering in from yet farther east, yet farther south. The results – recorded by Pliny and Solinus and manipulated by later marvel-mongers like Mandeville – made hair-raising reading. Mandeville described a land 'where the folk be great giants of twenty-eight foot long, or thirty foot long . . . And they eat more gladly man's flesh than any other flesh'. And further north there were 'full cruel and evil women. And they have precious stones in their eyes. And they be of that kind that if they behold any man with wrath they slay him anon with the beholding, as doth the basilisk'. There were rivers where flashing waters turned out to be precious stones, but others beside whose banks the crocodile, as he gulped down a passing stranger, visibly wept.

They were lands of untold wealth, and insupportable perils. And it was all so circumstantial! Here is Mandeville describing the Pismires, who quarry gold from the hills of Taprobane and eat any human they see. In spite of this hazard, 'the folk of the country get gold by this subtlety . . . They take mares that have young colts or foals, and lay upon the mares void [empty] vessels made therefor, and they be all open above and hanging low to the earth. And then they send forth those mares for to pasture about those hills and withhold the foals with them at home. And when the Pismires see those vessels, they leap in anon. And they have this kind [habit] that they let nothing be empty among them, but anon they fill it, be it what manner of thing that it be. And so they fill those vessels with gold. And when that the folk suppose that the vessels be full, they put forth anon the young foals, and make them neigh after their dams. And then anon the mares return towards their foals with their charges of gold.'

There were Christian marvels, too. Somewhere in Darkest Africa ruled a Christian ruler, Prester John, of fabulous wealth and power but uncertain whereabouts. It was hoped until well into the sixteenth century that if only a European could get in touch with him, the conversion of Africa might be accomplished; a hope which, as he did not exist, was doomed to disappointment. In southern India there was believed to be a flourishing community of Christians founded by the Apostle Thomas. This too was a myth, but, like the story of Prester John, it created a bond of interest in a land otherwise infidel and hostile, and was strong enough to convince Vasco da Gama that the fanged Hindu deities he saw portrayed at Calicut were angels and saints.

But there was enough hard fact, and enough real need for gold and spices to maintain a constant pressure down the west coast. Henry and his successors inherited a crusading tradition, and their zeal in converting the heathen was sustained by a trade in slaves which began in Africa (it was already commonplace in Mediterranean ports) in 1441. Moreover the exploration of the coast did not involve, as did the discovery of America, an imaginative leap far into the dark. The bogies could be exorcised as seamen coasted south, approaching the unknown, cape by cape and beach by beach, from the security of the known. The closeness with which the ships hugged the coast as they advanced can be seen from the wealth of place-names given from the earliest days. The Italian Cadomosto, who captained a Portuguese vessel in 1455 to the river Gambia, explained that Cape Verde was so called because of its greenness, and Cape Bianco from the whiteness of its sands, and his companions named two rivers after the palms at the mouth of one and the smoke from native fires hanging over the other. In 1471 Elmina, the site of what was to be the most important fortress in West Africa, was reached, and in 1473 Lopo Gonçalves safely crossed the Equator.

The hope that India would be easy to reach, bolstered by the eastward trend of the Ivory, Gold and Slave Coasts beyond Cape Palmas, was given up as navigators were forced south again from

Fernando Po. But by this time there was another driving force in Portugal, John II, who came to the throne in 1481 and who, as a scholar, was encouraged by the increasing number of maps like Fra Mauro's which showed the longed-for sea route to the Indies and who, as monarch, could put more money into exploration than Prince Henry had been able to muster; he was, in addition, spurred by the increasing competitiveness of other nations.

Though little is known about them, it is clear that many expeditions sailed from Spain and that cargoes of West African slaves became a familiar quayside scene in Seville. The English were also showing an interest and indeed applied to the Papacy – which had given exclusive rights to Portugal – for permission to take part in the West African trade. John, aware that the gold supplies were disappointing, and anxious not to be forestalled in the goal which had overtaken that of African trade, sent his captains ever further south, instructing them as an added precaution to erect inscribed stone crosses – padrões – where they landed to stake an exclusive claim for Portugal. This urge to protect the staging posts on the way to the Indies was futile, for from Vasco da Gama onwards ships bound for the Indies did not hug the coast, with its fitful airs, but swung out westwards from Sierra Leone far into the south Atlantic in order to catch the prevailing north-westerlies to the Cape. But it encouraged the establishment of colonies, one of which, Angola, has been a source of pride and, possibly, profit to Portugal to this day.

John II was called by his countrymen 'the Perfect'. Certainly he was a perfectionist. His sea-captains were backed by a brains-trust far larger than the group of scholars mustered by Prince Henry. His ability to pick men was shown by the exploits of his squire, Diogo Cão, who reached Cape Cross, 22° south of the Equator, in 1485, and of Bartholomew Dias who, blown off the coast and driven far south and west by storms, doubled the Cape unawares and in his attempt to regain contact with the land got as far east as the Great Fish River in 1488. Dias called the Cape, with dour realism, the Cape of Storms, but John, realizing that Ptolemy had been disproved and his own experts proved right, re-named it the Cape of Good Hope. His thoroughness is shown by his despatching, in the same year that Dias left, an expedition in the opposite direction but with the same end: to investigate the possibility of a route to the Indies. While Dias probed the approach to the Indian Ocean from the west, Pero da Covilhan and Alfonso de Paiva were to see what information they could pick up on the east coast of Africa. They were to use local transport – Covilhan spoke fluent Arabic – and to pose as merchants.

Via Naples, Rhodes, Alexandria and Cairo they reached Aden, trading as they went. There they split up, Paiva setting off to get first-hand information about the extent of Ethiopia and the possibility of a Portuguese alliance, while Covilhan, like a state-sponsored Marco Polo, began a remarkable series of wanderings on both sides of the Indian Ocean, immersing himself in the thriving Moslem trade-world with a view to advising the king how best to break into it. He crossed to Calicut, worked up the Indian coast to Goa, crossed back to Ormuz and then – the most important part of his mission – sailed to Sofala, just south of the present Beira in Moçambique. Here he made inquiries about sea-routes round southern Africa and, probably from stories of Arab ships blown round from the east as Dias was blown round from the west, gathered that a circumnavigation was possible. This news, together with information about the Moslem–dominated spice trade between India and the Red Sea and Persian Gulf, he sent back to John in a letter written on his return to Cairo where he met two envoys sent to contact him by the King. The result of the Dias-Covilhan pincer movement was to identify, in a reasonably practicable manner, the whole African coastline with the exception of the stretch where the two did not quite touch hands between East London and Beira. The ground for Vasco da Gama's voyage round the Cape to Sofala and Calicut had been prepared and almost certainly it was only John's illness and death in 1495 that delayed Portuguese contact with the east.

These expeditions show that there was a fundamental difference between the exploration of Africa and that of Asia. The African coast had to be charted without assistance: the languages were all strange, there was no native coastal shipping that could be used south of Cape Verde, no native pilots to give advice. Once the Cape had been rounded, however, and contact made with Moçambique, Europeans entered a highly sophisticated trading area with maps, pilots and a busy traffic of large ships. The Indian Ocean resembled an Arabic-speaking Mediterranean and with interpreters from among the Arabs of Portugal and Spain Europeans could quickly master its intricacies. The hazards of distance, piracy and, on land, war, were greater than in Africa, but the navigational obstacles were fewer and the challenges to the imagination less daunting.

Another difference was that Europeans could explore the interior of Asia by joining merchant caravans or groups of pilgrims: the difficulty was not to find the routes but to gain permission to use them. In Africa south of the Sahara there were no pilgrimages to join, no well-beaten trade paths to tread. The only way to penetrate the interior was to make an expedition in force. A few such expeditions struck inland from the coast, as we shall see, but hostile natives, an inhospitable landscape, disease, and the absence of reasonably civilized towns or markets where men could recuperate meant that these expeditions did not penetrate far and that it was impossible for solitary travellers to cover enormous distances as they did in Asia.

There were, indeed, a number of free-lance European merchants already trading in the Indian Ocean, and the account of his ventures written in 1496 by a Genoese, Geronimo de Santo Stefano, shows both the possibilities and the hazards of this area.

Starting from Aden, some five years before Vasco da Gama reached Calicut, 'we embarked for India in another ship, fastened together with cords; the sails were made of cotton. We sailed for twenty-five days without seeing land, and then we saw numerous islands but did not touch at them, and continuing our voyage for ten days more until a favourable wind, we finally arrived at a great city called Calicut ... We departed hence in another ship, made like the one above described, and after a navigation of twenty-six days we arrived at a large island called Ceylon ... Departing thence after twelve days, we reached another place called Coromandel ... We departed hence in another ship and after twenty days reached a great city called Pegu [up-country from Rangoon]. This port is called Lower India [Burma]. Here is a great lord who possesses more than ten thousand elephants, and every year he breeds five hundred of them. This country is distant fifteen days' journey by land from another, called Ava [near Mandalay], in which grow rubies and many other precious stones. Our wish was to go to this place, but at that time the two princes were at war, so that no-one was allowed to go from the one place to the other. Thus we were compelled to sell the merchandise which we had in the said city of Pegu, which were of such a sort that only the lord of the city could purchase them . . . The price amounted to two thousand ducats, and as we wished to be paid we were compelled, by reason of the troubles and intrigues occasioned by the aforesaid war, to remain there a year and a half, all of which time we had daily to solicit at the house of the said lord . . . I set sail in a ship to go to Malacca, and after being on the sea twenty-five days, one morning, in not very favourable weather, we reached a very large island called Sumatra . . . Finding that this was not a desirable place to stay in, I determined to take my departure, and selling all my merchandise, I converted the value into silk and benzoin [aromatic gum] and set sail in a ship to return to Cambay [at the head of the Bay of Cambay], and after being twenty-five days at sea in unfavourable weather, we reached certain islands called the Maldives . . . We were obliged to stay here six months.' Then, after losing all his goods by shipwreck, he managed to struggle to Cambay and home via Ormuz.

This bald narrative gives a sufficiently vivid picture of European activity in the East before the Portuguese 'discovered' it. Santo Stefano was able to get himself and his tradegoods across the Arabian Sea; from south-west India round Cape Comorin to Ceylon; and then via south-east India across the Bay of Bengal to Burma. After that he got to the Malaysian spice *entrepôt*, Malacca, where junks from China and the Moluccas trans-shipped their wares to the Moslem dhows, and so, though disastrously, back to the Mediterranean. The contrast between conditions east and west of Sofala, the southern limit of this sophisticated trade area, is striking. Equally striking is that Santo Stefano and his nameless colleagues were parasites on it, not masters of it.

Parasitism began to give way to mastery as soon as Vasco da Gama's ships got past Sofala. One of John II's last actions had been to name da Gama – like Cão and Dias and Covilhan a member of his own household, in daily contact with the king's geographers, map-makers and mathematicians – for the command of an expedition to follow the trail blazed by Dias and Covilhan. But it was left to John's successor Manuel to organize the expedition, and from its success the Portuguese have known him as 'The Fortunate' ever since. The planning was in the tradition of Henry and John. Dias was the practical adviser, supervising the design of two of the four ships, the *St. Gabriel* and the *St. Raphael* of between 100–120 tons, and suggesting routes. Maps were specially prepared and so were reports (like Covilhan's) on what da Gama might expect to find, new astronomical instruments and tables of declination for using the sun once the pole star had been left behind. Some of Dias' own men were among the crews, and Dias himself accompanied the fleet for its first lap down the West African coast, turning his caravel east to Elmina when da Gama swung out westwards to catch the winds that would drive him to the Cape. Both the *St. Gabriel* (the flagship) and *St. Raphael* were fitted out for defence and well armed: they were, after all, out to break the age's greatest monopoly. To them, Manuel added a small (50 tons) and swift lateener, the *Berrio*, for use as scout and messenger, and a storeship of about 200–250 tons. Each sail was painted with the red cross of the Order of Christ, and at the dedication service da Gama was given a banner with the same device while Manuel reminded the captains of the two-fold object of their voyage: to take Christ to the East, and to bring profits back to the West.

With so long a tradition of carefully sifted information, with such scrupulous preparation, in which money was not spared and the most up-to-date scientific knowledge recruited, it is tempting to see da Gama's voyage as the prose version of Columbus' more modest, more ramshackle and (by our maps, if not by his) more uncertain venture of five years before. These two voyages are the most famous of all time, they have been fully and repeatedly described, and there is a sense in which the historian, while setting the scene and estimating the consequences, should step back and leave the narrative to the survivors, to poets and to other seamen. One-third of da Gama's crews perished. From leaving the Cape Verde islands to their anchorage one hundred and thirty miles north of the Cape of Good Hope they had been out of sight of land for ninety-six days. This may well have been the result of a last consultation before Dias left the fleet; by skirting the storm areas he had battled with, da Gama discovered the wind route between Europe and the Cape which has been followed by sailing ships ever after. Or it may be that other mariners had reported on the wind systems of the South Atlantic: there are fragmentary references to knowledge of Brazil before the 'authoritative' date of 1500 when Pedro Alvarez Cabral landed there.

Rather than limp along the scanty stepping stones which the contemporary records (muzzled in the interest of secrecy) provide of da Gama's progress around South Africa to his contact with the Moslem world at Moçambique, I would refer the reader to the epic poem of which da Gama is the hero, Camoens' *The Lusiads*. Camoens himself had made the voyage to India in 1553. He knew its hazards; of the four ships of his flotilla only one got safely round the Cape and across to Goa. Patriotism, ruthless religiosity, the glamour of adventure and fear of the unknown: it is best to leave these components of our story to a poet of genius who was close to the gossip, knew the men and was at the heart of the mood of the first generation of Portuguese enterprise in the Indian Ocean.

And because the sources communicate little of the hazards of this outward voyage, let a later seaman, an Englishman, writing in 1579, speak for the Portuguese as they worked against the westward set of the current off Cape Agulhas. 'The wind turning south, and the waves being exceeding great, rolled us so near the land that the ship stood in less than fourteen fathoms of water, no more than six miles from the Cape, which is called Das Agulias, and there we stood as utterly cast away, for under us were rocks of main stone so sharp and cutting that no anchor could hold the ship, the shore so evil that nothing could land, and the land itself so full of tigers and people that are savage and killers of all strangers that we had no hope of life, nor comfort but only in God and a good conscience. Notwithstanding, after we had lost anchor, hoisting up the sails for to get the ship a coast in some safer place, or when it should please God, it pleased his mercy suddenly, where no man looked for help, to fill our sails with wind from the land, and so we escaped.'

At Moçambique, da Gama entered a world where, as navigator,

he was no longer a pioneer. In the harbour there were large merchant ships and their Arab pilots used the compass, the astrolabe and the quadrant – instruments indeed which their medieval ancestors had introduced to the Mediterranean and which the Portuguese now ironically brought full circle to use against them. From this point, however, da Gama needed other talents, those of the diplomat and soldier. He had to fight his way out of Moçambique, watch a captured and quite naturally treacherous pilot like a hawk on the way up to Mombasa, escape from a trap laid for him there and negotiate carefully at Malindi, further north, for a trustworthy pilot to take him across to India.

Before accompanying him to Calicut, safe at last in the hands of the Gujerati Ibn Majid, we may pause for a moment to consider his achievement, and take a last look at the Renaissance exploration of Africa. In comparison to Columbus, da Gama's task was at once easier and more demanding. Easier because it did not involve the leap into the dark, the blind trust in geographical theory that the discovery of America involved; the only 'new' ground covered by da Gama was the stretch of waste between Dias' last anchorage in Mossel Bay and Moçambique. But the distance he had to cover, the seamanship necessary to make his landfall near the Cape after the three month sweep out into the Atlantic, and to battle against the fierce currents running against him off Cape Agulhas (one of the reasons why the nerve of Dias' men had been broken) and off Moçambique: these factors support his claim to be at least Columbus' equal as a mariner. As a practical navigator, Columbus' uncanny ability to feel his way back repeatedly to a given landfall puts him in a class of his own. On the theoretical side, however, da Gama was much his superior as the charts and maps, which represent their discoveries, show. To follow Columbus' latitudes resulted in errors of more than ten degrees, while the Cantino map which followed those of da Gama contains no error in the African coastline of as much as two degrees.

When da Gama sailed from Malindi, the Renaissance exploration of the African coast was to all intents and purposes finished. In 1500 one of the ships from the next Portuguese expedition, driven off course after leaving Moçambique, discovered Madagascar, and later in the century detailed surveys were made of the South African coast. But this was to protect vessels from shipwreck by providing them with detailed charts, not to find new trading posts or establish links with Prester John. By this time, the glamour of the wealth of the Americas, of India and the East Indies had relegated South and East Africa to the status of staging-posts; only in West Africa was there enough easy profit to pick up from ivory and slaves to ensure a steady international bickering.

Exploration of the interior was to wait for the colonial and missionary rivalry of the industrial age. The Portuguese left a shallowly Europeanized Kingdom of the Congo behind them – Cão had manoeuvred his ships one hundred miles up-river – and a fair number of Portuguese emigrated to Angola and traded with the upland regions. In 1514, Antonio Fernandes travelled up-country from Sofala, across Mashonaland and into the regions ruled by the Monomotapa, ruler of the land between Salisbury and the Zambesi which legend held to be the seat of a civilization rich in gold. Almost nothing is known about this journey and it was not followed up. The Portuguese set up fortified posts on the Zambesi itself later in the century, and from one of these, Tete, Gaspar Bocarro went north-west to Kilwa, discovering Lake Nyasa, but the only region inside Africa that became reasonably well-known was Ethiopia, where a series of expeditions, still half hoping to find and enlist the crusading zeal of Prester John, prepared the way for a Jesuit mission which arrived in 1557 and stayed for forty years. Another missionary, Manuel d'Almeida, almost certainly deserves the credit for being the discoverer of the source of the Blue Nile in 1613, and from his experience of the torrential rains in the highlands of Ethiopia, he became the first man to explain the inundations of the Nile which had puzzled geographers since antiquity.

The Indian port in which da Gama at last dropped anchor was Calicut. We have seen that he was by no means the first European to visit the Malabar coast. Covilhan had found Venetians and Genoese, French and Dutchmen who had been drawn there by trade or *wanderlust*, using the craft that trafficked regularly from Cairo down the Red Sea and along the easy wind route to West India. These men were too few and too unco-ordinated to present a challenge to the Arabs and Persians who ran the coastal trade, but their presence alerted Moslem jealousy at the sight of an organized expedition sent by a European King. It was only after threading a maze of intrigue and using force that the Portuguese were able to obtain a somewhat meagre cargo for the return voyage. But from the moment when da Gama's cinnamon and ginger, cloves and pepper, nutmeg and precious stones arrived at Lisbon a shock-wave of alarm spread among the Mediterranean ports which saw their spice-trade by-passed, and Manuel lost no time in proclaiming himself 'Lord of the conquest, navigation and commerce of Ethiopia, Arabia, Persia and India' and making plans for annual expeditions to the east.

Less than a year after Vasco da Gama's return the King dispatched Pedro Alvarez Cabral with a merchant fleet of thirteen sail, and the history of the Indian Ocean for the next fifty years becomes less the story of its exploration than its exploitation by the merchants, the seamen and the military governors of Portugal. The creation, by a nation so far away, and so small – the population of Portugal was probably well under two million – of a virtual monopoly of trade in the Arabian sea is one of the most daring and glamorous episodes in the history of the Renaissance. From a string of fortified ports in West India, Cochin, Goa and Diu among them, Portuguese vessels sailed across to the Malabar coast and back round the Cape, protected from Arab raiders by ships based on Ormuz and Mombasa. But the skill with which the Portuguese took advantage of the political rivalry between the coastal potentates in India, the vigour of their seamanship which defeated the great fleets that tried to break their hold on the carrying trade, the skill of their engineers who constructed the brilliantly designed fortifications which can still be seen in Goa, at Diu, in East Africa and as far up the Persian Gulf as Bahrain – all these factors are outside the purpose of this book.

The Portuguese entry into the Indian Ocean was more in the nature of an occupation than an exploration. They took over existing knowledge rather than extended it. They were forced, of course, to make charts and compile navigational handbooks, but they were drawing as much on local information as on their own observation: their portrait of the geography of the Ocean was a translation rather than an original work. In India, they pursued an orthodox policy of power, alternately bullying and cajoling the Hindus, fraternising as much as possible with Moslem traders on land and killing them remorselessly at sea; lacking both the incentive, and sufficient troops, to strike inland, the exploration of mainland India was left to individuals, travelling not for the Crown but to satisfy their own curiosity or sense of divine purpose. And even when we do hear of sixteenth century travellers penetrating the interior, encouraged by the religious tolerance of the Mogul empire, they go primarily as missionaries or cultivated tourists rather than as discoverers, and are content to accompany the polite and learned court of Akbar and his successors from Delhi to Agra and to the elegant capital they were building at Fatehpur Sikri. Not till 1602 did a traveller, the Jesuit Benedict Goes, leave Agra for Afghanistan, and work round, north of the Himalayas, to China. In 1624, another Jesuit, Antonio de Andrade made a journey from Agra into Tibet, the first European known to have crossed the Himalayas. The exploration of India south of the heartland of the Mogul Empire had to wait till the coming of European colonial activity in the eighteenth century.

It was indeed almost the same with India as it had been with Africa: the Portuguese, once they had secured trading bases there, transferred their exploring zeal to the true *raison d'être* of the Indian Ocean trade: the Moluccas, the Spice Islands themselves. In these seas late medieval maps were unhelpful. Some merchants' gossip about the Malay peninsula and the East Indies has been picked up in Europe in antiquity and during the middle ages, but the maps either confused them together in a huge peninsula reaching south-east of India or put in a random scattering of islands whose names and positions bore no relation to what seamen actually found. As in the case of India, individual merchants had traded as far afield as Indonesia, but, without cartographic knowledge themselves, their information was too vague to be of use to map-makers in Europe.

The achievements of the first generation of the sixteenth century can be seen by comparing the far eastern part of the Cantino map of 1502 with that of Diogo Ribeiro's world map of 1527. On the Cantino map India and Ceylon appear already with tolerable accuracy, but Malaysia and the Indonesian islands are conflated into a giant promontory, several times the size of India, with Sumatra lying off it to the west, about right for size, but oriented north-east south-west instead of north-west south-east. By 1527, the formidable task of fragmenting this great bulk of guesswork into its component parts was well advanced.

How it was done cannot be reconstructed in detail here. The area was the flash-point of Spanish-Portuguese rivalry. The attempt on the part of the Portuguese to maintain secrecy, though backed by capital punishment for offenders, was not entirely successful: recently returned seamen are compulsive gossips (many of them transferred to the service of foreign powers) and all cartographical departments were liable to infiltration by spies: the record is maimed, nevertheless. The task was eased, as in the case of the Indian Ocean, by the existence of an organized trade, centred on Malacca but reaching up to the precious stones and ivory of Siam, the superb weapons of Japan, and, most important, the spices of the Moluccas. East of Malacca this trade was in the hands of Chinese and Japanese, westwards and north it was controlled by Arabs and Persians, by Parsees from Gujerat and Chattis from Madras. There was information to be gleaned here, and from Indonesian pilots themselves; when a chart of Indonesia of Javanese origin was obtained in 1511 the viceroy of India, Albuquerque, triumphantly declared it 'the best thing I have seen!' In addition to these sources of information, expeditions were sent out to explore from India and, after its occupation by the Portuguese in 1511, from Malacca, like that of Antonio de Abreu and Francisco Serrão. They visited Java and got among the Spice Islands themselves at Amboina and Banda. Serrão was shipwrecked – only too common an occurrence in those shoaling and reef-strewn waters – but reached Ternate in a native boat.

The difficulty of distinguishing one island from another and the problems that arose from inter-island rivalry made accurate charting intensely difficult, and complicating the task of the official cartographers in Lisbon, who had to combine the reports of formal expeditions with information derived from shipwrecked sailors and from native charts using unfamiliar conventions, was a matter that gave the mapping of this area an especial urgency: the impossibility of computing longitude at this period.

44

We shall see in the next chapter that in 1494 the Treaty of Tordesillas gave newly discovered lands west of 46° 37' west of Greenwich (translating the award into modern terms) to Spain, and those discovered east of this latitude to Portugal. A line of longitude, of course, runs right round the world, and both sides hoped that it gave the Moluccas to them. In fact the islands fell within Portugal's hemisphere, but because the computation of longitude required an accurate chronometer, and time was then measured by hour-glasses, there was no certainty, and until 1529, when Charles V sold his claim over the Spice Islands to Portugal for 350,000 ducats, sorely needed for his vast commitments in Europe, there was constant wrangling and fighting on the frontier where, half the globe across, two world powers grappled at the limits of their communications for mastery.

It was with this in mind that Camoens, when describing the stirring embarkation of da Gama from Lisbon, introduces an old man, who speaks across the widening gap between the ships and the shore:

'Oh, the folly of it, this craving for power, this thirsting after the vanity we call fame . . . To what new perils is it bent on leading this realm and its people? What perils and deaths has it in store for them, concealed under some fair-sounding name? . . . You allow the enemy to flourish at your gates while you go seek another at the other side of the world, at the price of depopulating and weakening this ancient kingdom and squandering its resources. You are lured by the perils of the uncertain and the unknown, to the end that fame may exalt and flatter you, proclaiming you with a wealth of titles lords of India, Persia, Arabia and Ethiopia. A curse on him who first launched on the waters a barque with sails!'

3
The Americas

In the exploration of Africa and the east, the voyagers were correcting guesses, proving and disproving theories, bending the conjectured outlines of the maps nearer to their real shape. Africa, the Indian Ocean, Malaysia and Indonesia, the Spice Islands: at the end of the fifteenth century there was general agreement that these all existed, the problem was to arrange them into a usable pattern. But westwards the situation was quite different. No one suspected the existence of the American continent. No maps, no geographical theory left room for it. From Ptolemy onwards men had underestimated the girth of the world and exaggerated the east-west length of Asia: two factors that made the Ocean Sea perilously wide but not so vast that the imagination wished to put a continent in it – an imagination that, in the absence of positive evidence to the contrary, expressed both its *horror vacui* and its conviction that God at the Creation was more concerned with the land and with man than with the sea and leviathan, kept the ocean as a mere decorative border on the map. Two of the books studied by Columbus, the *Travels* of Marco Polo and the *Imago Mundi* (c. 1410) of Cardinal Pierre d'Ailly, both shrank the Ocean Sea and stretched Asia towards Europe. Toscanelli, the foremost mathematician-cosmographer of Columbus' day, put the distance between the Atlantic and Asian coasts at 5,000 miles, some 7,000 shorter than the real distance, and Columbus himself, the most persuasive salesman of the short-sea approach to Cathay, by re-estimating the length of a degree on the equator and scaling it down to the latitude he intended to sail along (28° north), came to a total of 3,500 miles; he thus dragged Japan (the Cipangu which Marco Polo had placed well east of China–Cathay) to the actual longitude of the Virgin Islands. It was fortunate that America did exist to cover him from the consequences of this colossal miscalculation.

It is this quality of total unexpectedness that gives the story of American discovery so much of its fascination. All that men did expect to find *en route* to Cathay were islands. The Faroes and Iceland had been reached from Ireland in the eighth century and contact with them was maintained throughout the middle ages. Using the broad, partly-decked Kaup-ship, the Norwegians had reached Greenland by the middle of the tenth century and by the middle of the thirteenth century there were well over five thousand settlers there. From Greenland expeditions – or ships blown off course – had discovered Baffin Island, Labrador and the still uncertain point on the coast of New England which the sagas called Vinland. But there was no suggestion that there was continental land in the north-west Atlantic; the mainland contact is shown on the Yale map as 'Vinlanda Insula'. Further south, as we have seen, other islands were discovered: the Madeiras, the Canaries and the Azores.

In addition to these real islands, the maps showed a variety of imaginary ones. One of them, the island of Brazil, was not expunged from Admiralty charts until 1865. Somewhere, it was thought, was Atlantis, or the Fortunate Islands, that vanished civilization mentioned by Plato and kept alive in the writings of medieval geographers. West of Ireland there was the island named after its alleged discoverer, St. Brandon. These isles of fable (but vouched for by cartographers) were the result of pure myth plus the sighting of fogbanks or horizon cloud by fishermen blown west from their home waters by storm, but they were present in Columbus' mind's eye when he wrote in mid-Atlantic on his first voyage that he was sure that his ships were 'going through between' them. Islands were stressed in the instructions given by the Spanish monarchs to Columbus: 'You, Christopher Columbus, are going by our orders to discover and gain, with certain ships of ours and with our men, certain islands and mainland in the Ocean Sea, and it is hoped that with the aid of God there shall be gained some of the said islands and mainland.' In this context 'mainland' could only mean Cathay, home of the Great Khan, greatest of all non-Christian potentates, on whose good will the Spaniards would have to rely in negotiating for the gold and spices of the Indies. The fact that Columbus was given three small ships, one, the *Santa Maria*, manned by ex-convicts, no letters of credence or presents of the kind normally exchanged between princes, and a minimum of armament: all this suggests that the Catholic Kings were more preoccupied with the island stepping-stones than with the continental terminus. Short as Columbus claimed the route to Cathay to be, there were clearly reservations about its practicability among Isabella's circle of advisers; islands, however, might well be found, and their inhabitants might provide information about the mainland beyond them. It was not until Columbus returned with the claim that he had reached an island group off the coast of Cathay itself that he was invited to return with an expedition planned on a large scale.

This vision of a wide sea, sprinkled with islands, reaching without interruption from Spain to Cathay is as near that we can get to the truth on the eve of Columbus' first voyage in 1492. The uncertainty is so great that claims to have forestalled him have been made on behalf of Basque and French seamen, of Welshmen and Portuguese, even for ships from China and fourteenth century Guinea. None can be substantiated. What is not in doubt is that there was a growing conviction during the fifteenth century that the western ocean was navigable and offered a practicable route to Cathay. 'This sea,' d'Ailly had written, 'is navigable in a few days if the wind is favourable.' The conviction was based on Ptolemy's estimate of distance, buttressed by the discovery of the middle Atlantic island groups, and by the practical experience of seamen: Portuguese who had learned to counter the north-east trades when returning from Africa or the Azores by bearing far out to the north-west before setting course for home; French and English fishermen reaching far towards the north-west. From 1480, indeed, small expeditions had been financed from Bristol to find the mythical island of Brazil, and in 1497 John Cabot touched the mainland, probably at Newfoundland. The Portuguese may have been making similar thrusts into the west towards Brazil. A chart in Bianco's Atlas (1436) has 'here is the

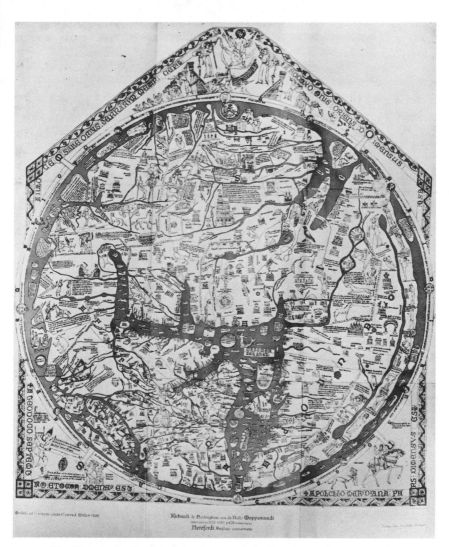

The Hereford Map: A Jerusalem map or *Mappamundi* of Richard of Haldingham: drawn between 1276 and 1285 and preserved in Hereford Cathedral. A map for contemplation, not for use. See page 14. *Radio Times Hutton Picture Library.*

Wood-engraving from Columbus' letter published in 1493: not a 'portrait' of his *Santa Maria,* but a fair representation of a common type of explorer's ship. *The Mansell Collection.*

Two wood-engravings of fabulous creatures reproduced from the Nuremberg Chronicle of 1493: figure with enormous foot based on a miniature from *Le Livre des Merveilles* of 1375. On the persistence of a belief in monsters, see page 32. *British Museum*.

Aden: early sixteenth-century woodcut. It was from Aden that intrepid merchants and travellers took shipping for India even before its 'discovery' by Vasco da Gama. See page 36. *British Museum.*

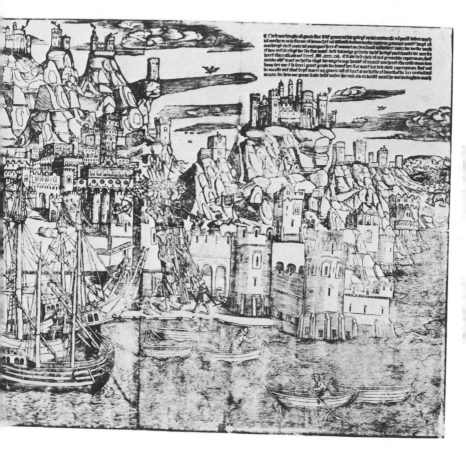

¶ Oeste waert seghet eß groote stat Alst gheuoecht hier ghelegē en dit contlrecht en geen ander maeck nō werste in so bestoruet en bewaecht en wstilandt baeden berghe capteyns gemoeret waert hoegt eß waerberegi ein sē moric wt passegaert here ein mornet, ein Druchland wpstelldert maect her werde waert eß hier weste riegt hier die stat waent heer batartge geluecht op dū berghe parchuwande wt waer ghe hierē ein sē waerh als mē ein berrel wal .M. .cccc. xiii. ein eß also deze stede nō werst gemeeldtbe capteyneus, sind werste alse waert werht de riegt die engelsouge bemdē ein wuendē ein ein berrel eße stelds waent hier hoep her ein ein sen berrel gesel gesāte die bande her stat waert dat deze stede capteynman sind wel be moeste stilt stuut keyst waert ein gauert last eß saeet al werberste en bnoelst dar deze bestud dael sagen. Die herm oer groote stade beulst andet ligt wael ale die berstt memse her wel berlaghten waert.

Miniature showing a mariner taking a bearing: from a navigational treatise of 1583 by Jacques de Vaulx in the *Bibliothèque Nationale, Paris.* This angle-and-bearing device reflects the aspirations of shore-based experts rather than the actual practice of mariners. See page 96.

Mariner's compass: probably Italian; ivory; 16th century. 4½″ diameter: in the *National Maritime Museum, London.* The most important instrument used in navigation. See page 97.

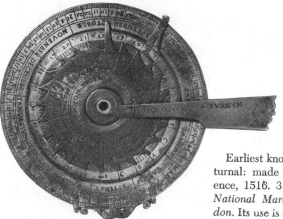

Earliest known example of a nocturnal: made by Vulporia of Florence, 1516. 3¾" diameter: in the *National Maritime Museum, London*. Its use is described on page 90.

Pocket brass quadrant: 16th century: in the *Science Museum, London*. For the use of this instrument, see page 96.

Planispheric astrolabe: German, 15th century. It was on sophisticated land instruments like this that the simpler versions used at sea were developed. See page 96. *Science Museum, London*.

Gerardus Mercator: world map, 1538. See page 71.

57

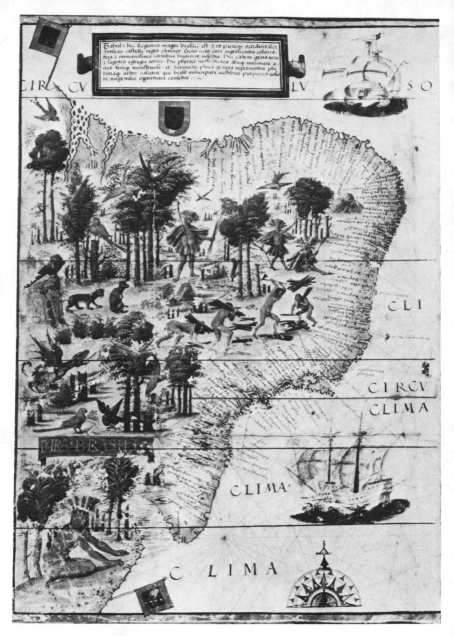

Portuguese chart of the South Atlantic: from the Miller Atlas, *c.* 1519. In the *Bibliothèque Nationale, Paris.* A typical blend of accuracy and exotic fantasy.

Section of portolan chart of 1547. A glamourized portrayal of Cartier's landing in Canada in 1534; the accurate-seeming coastline is largely guesswork. *Henry E. Huntington Library and Art Gallery.*

Their rype corne

Their greene corne

Corne newly sprong

Their sitting at meate

The howse wherin the Tombe of their Herounds standeth

Prayer

SECOTON·

A Ceremony in their prayers ye
strange gestures and songes dansing
about posts carued on the topps
lyke mens faces.

Watercolour by John White (*c.* 1590) of the Indian settlement of
Secoton, Virginia. White was one of the pioneer settlers on Roanoke Island,
North Carolina, and was also a pioneer of straightforward observation.
British Museum.

sea of weeds' at its western border, and the vigour with which John II of Portugal fought to preserve Portuguese rights over the south-west Atlantic during the negotiations leading to the Treaty of Tordesillas in 1494 suggests that contact may have been made with South America well before then.

With this background, it is perhaps surprising that Columbus spent so many weary years selling 'The Enterprise of the Indies'. John refused to help, and it was long before Spain decided to support him. But the background was concerned with islands; it was islands that the Bristolians were seeking; the first recorded report of Brazil (the mainland Brazil) by Caminha in 1500 assumed that it was an island. Columbus' project, however, was to make contact with the Asian mainland: it may well have seemed that he was proposing to run before he could walk. And there was a further obstacle in his way. That he was an experienced seaman, there is no doubt. He knew the Mediterranean (he was born in Genoa, second only to Venice among the trading powers of Italy), he had been to Elmina, possibly to Iceland, he knew the Middle Atlantic islands – had, indeed, married the daughter of the governor of Porto Santo, Madeira, where he spent several years. He was an accomplished navigator and chart-maker and was familiar with the scholarly literature about cosmography. But he was obscure and he was poor, and he was intensely ambitious. He was not simply asking permission to verify a theory, he was asking to be given the chance of becoming the wealthiest and most influential private individual in Europe. Columbus was convinced that the westward route was practicable, and if he had merely wished for an opportunity to test that theory he could have done so, in all probability, by getting backing from a group of merchants. The sum raised for his voyage was, in fact, small, and none came directly from government funds. But he wanted more, far more than to satisfy his curiosity and blaze a trail for others. Just how much he demanded is shown in the patent eventually granted him before he left on his first voyage. Whatever territories he discovered, the patent ran, 'you shall be our Admiral and Viceroy and Governor of them, and thereafter may call and entitle yourself Don Christopher Columbus and so may your sons and successors . . . forever and always'. He was also to have a tenth of the profits of all the spices, precious stones, gold and other products the new lands might contain. His demands were, indeed, staggering; a title of nobility, a crown office, and a tenth of the fabled riches of Cathay. How he obtained what was potentially the largest contract on record is not known but its negotiation must have been prolonged – and it had, of course, to be broken when the scope of his discoveries was realized.

We do know something of the arguments he used, however, for he recapitulated them in a later letter to Ferdinand and Isabella. If they would trust his reasoning, both God and mammon would be served. 'I gave to the subject six or seven years of great anxiety, explaining, to the best of my ability, how great service might be done to our Lord by promulgating his sacred name and our holy faith among so many nations; an enterprise exalted in itself and calculated to enhance the glory and immortalize the renown of the greatest sovereigns. It was also requisite to refer to the temporal prosperity which was foretold in the writings of so many trustworthy and wise historians who related that great riches were to be found in those parts. And at the same time I thought it desirable to bring to bear upon the subject the sayings and opinions of those who have written upon the geography of the world.'

1492 was the year in which Lorenzo de'Medici died, Roderigo Borgia began, as Alexander VI, what was to be the most notorious of all papal reigns, and the conquest of Granada concluded the centuries-long crusade against the Moors of Spain. But none of these events can compare in significance with the discoveries made by the three ships, *Santa Maria* (about 120 tons), *Nina* and *Pinta* (about 60 tons each), which left Palos on August 3rd. After a month of reprovisioning and some alteration of sail plan in the Canaries, Columbus led them due west on the latitude, 28° N., where his maps showed Cipangu and its islands lying like a shield before the mainland of Cathay.

Physically, this was one of the most routine of explorers' voyages. The weather was fair, the winds steady: on their best day the fleet made one hundred and eighty miles, not much less than the run of the smaller tramp steamers of today. After thirty-three days Watling Island, a somewhat mournful outrider of the Bahamas group, was sighted. There was an ample supply of stores, not a sail was split, the last few days had been encouraged by sightings of weed and flocks of birds – known by all seamen to be signs of land. It had all gone as Columbus had foreseen, and he noted in his journal his intention to move on at once to Cipangu itself.

Instead of continuing to the west, however, he threaded his way south through the Bahamas, naming them as he went, straining to interpret the gestures and strange words of the inhabitants as signs that he was reaching the court of one of the great princes of the east, dropping continually southwards in the belief – shared by many in his age – that gold, which was the colour of the sun, would be found where the sun's rays burned most fiercely. And it was gold, above all, that Columbus was seeking. Reaching Cuba, with its mountainous interior and, after five weeks exploration, seemingly endless coastline, he decided first that this was Cipangu and then, after carefully computing his position on the maps which reflected the shrunken world of his own theories and the extended Asia of his fellow geographers, he concluded that Cuba was none other than the mainland of Cathay itself, albeit a region less wealthy and less sophisticated than the areas known to Marco Polo. Thus fortified by science, and, more sensitive than most of his contemporaries to natural beauty, delighted by the scents and sights of the sub-tropical zone, he saw himself as the discoverer both of the real world of Marco Polo and the fabulous world of Mandeville and the other marvel-mongers. Not far away, he wrote, was a land 'where there were one-eyed people and others with dog faces who ate people'. And further south was the island of martial women which had long been one of the most popular of fables: the empire of the Amazons. Not far from the point of Cuba-Cathay which he had reached was a province where men were born with tails. From all the evidence, then, except that of his quadrant reading of the north star, which put him in the latitude of Cape Cod and he discounted, he had done what he set out to do. Nor did the discovery of Haiti, in the following weeks, disturb him. It was natural that there should be islands off the Cathayan coast, and the small pieces of gold he obtained from the natives there confirmed that he was within the commercial empire of the Great Khan.

This conclusion, plus the shipwreck of the *Santa Maria*, led him to return. It was a voyage on which Columbus the dreamer, the visionary whose greed to be right led him to interpret everything he read or saw or heard as confirming his own convictions, was replaced by Columbus the inspired practical sea-dog. The end of the voyage, both before reaching the Azores, where he sheltered, and before arriving in Lisbon, was marked by long and terrible storms. Columbus came before Ferdinand and Isabella not only as a man who had proved a theory but as the man who could be trusted, for courage and skill, to follow up and exploit it for the glory and profit of Spain.

Columbus' gold samples were not impressive, but they were an indication of more to come. The natives he had brought back were physically quite different from any seen before in a country with a wide cross-section of slaves from Africa. Clearly they must be from Asia, the first visitors to Europe from Cathay. All this was a monstrous error, but a necessary one. Spain wanted specie and spices, not coconuts and Arawaks, and if Columbus had not decked out the primitive West Indies with the glamour of Cathay, Spain might never have sent out the expeditions which, by aiming to traffic with the old world, revealed the existence of the new.

Preparations for a second voyage were started at once, and Spain began negotiations for the most impressive monuments to Columbus' powers of persuasion, the papal bull *Inter Caetera* of 1493 and the Treaty of Tordesillas of the following June. Debilitated by national rivalry, the papacy retained some prestige – i.e. some usefulness – as a supra-national arbitrator. In 1454, when Portuguese exploration of the West African coast was beginning to look promising, the Crown had obtained bulls granting them a monopoly 'in the Ocean Sea towards the regions lying southward and eastwards' – south, that is, of the Canaries and east to the Indies. Now Spain asked permission to possess whatever she came across in her approaches to the Indies and to exclude all other nations from lands discovered west of a longitudinal line drawn three hundred miles out from the Azores. Haunted by the notion of an Ocean Sea different in kind from off-shore waters, Columbus had sensed a difference in the nature of the winds and the water at this point, and it was on his suggestion that Pope Alexander VI – conveniently a Spaniard himself – was asked to confirm this invisible frontier in the waves.

By *Inter Caetera* he granted to Spain 'all the islands and mainlands, found or to be found, discovered or to be discovered, westward or southward, by drawing and establishing a line running from the Arctic to the Antarctic Pole one hundred leagues west and south from any of the islands that are commonly called the Azores and Cape Verde'. A glance at the map shows that Alexander was making Spain a present of the Americas, but of this, of course, he can have had no conception; he was merely saying to two contenders for the Indies: you go this way, you go that. Manuel, however, was by now convinced that something existed south and west of his horizontal line (as the discovery of Brazil was shortly to prove) and demanded that it should not be pre-empted to the west by Spain's vertical line. The result was the Compromise of Tordesillas, whereby Spain retained her longitudinal division but shifted it further west to 46° 37', a shift which did secure Brazil to Portugal. Bizarre as this global carve-up, this last papal gesture in the large medieval manner, may seem (though we have seen proposals to map spheres of influence in outer space), it did serve to keep Portuguese and Spanish enterprise from conflict even if the other powers, who entered the mainstream of exploration at a later stage, took no notice of it. Its main contribution to the pace of exploration lay, as we have seen, on the other side of the world where the Tordesillas line plunged among the spice islands.

These negotiations produced a new and charged atmosphere; da Gama had not yet reached India, Cathay was as remote as ever, but Columbus had glimpsed what he thought was his quarry, and the hunt was up. Experts argued with new confidence, the gap between the bookish cosmographer and the thrusting world of commerce and diplomacy was narrowed, ideas were translated into action in sharp contrast to the years when Columbus had pointed in vain to the pregnant suggestions of d'Ailly and Toscanelli. Columbus himself made three more voyages, in 1493, 1498 and 1502. In 1498 another Spanish expedition sailed for the West Indies, in 1499 there were four. There may have been others in this period of which we have no record, certainly there were sailings among the islands which led to fresh discoveries. The pace was growing: it was in 1497 that John Cabot reached Labrador, and in 1498 that da Gama found at Calicut goods that had undoubtedly come from Cathay, silks, porcelains and spices far more convincing than the cassava and the barbaric accoutrements of the Arawaks. By 1500 all the major islands of the Antilles had been discovered and some thousand miles of the northern coastline of South America. Already the notion that this could not be Cathay was gaining currency. But not with Columbus. While the cosmographers of Italy, Portugal and England were making room in their picture of the globe for an as yet unnamed America, and there were increasing doubts among the Spaniards themselves, Columbus clung to the consequences of his original estimates of distance and fenced his imagination with the golden oval of the Caribbean. Perhaps he had not found the empire of the Great Khan – the doubt may well have crossed his mind as he moved among the gentle, scantily clad Tainos and the cannibal Carribs – what matter? Here there was gold, gold for himself and for the crown, and whereas in Cathay there would be knowing merchants and a trade world in which he would be a mere interloper, here there were no rivals and a population whose tameness and lack of armament marked them out to be slaves: living machinery to work the source of all these nuggets and ornaments he found in such profusion – if he could but find it.

Voyage by voyage, the evidence becomes clearer that Columbus was not interested in breaking out of his dream world of wealth. In 1494 he sailed along the south coast of Cuba to within some sixty miles of Cape San Antonio, its western tip, a voyage among shoals and cays that proved him a dogged master of coastal, as well as deep-sea navigation. But at that point, at Bahia Cortes, the coast began to turn to the south and Columbus stopped. Still convinced that Cuba was an eastward projecting promontory of the Chinese mainland, he interpreted the south-trending coast as the beginning of the huge peninsula called on contemporary maps the Golden Chersonese (in reality an elephantine guess at the Malay Peninsula). In contrast to the lands he had already found, where, according to the second fleet's physician Diego Chanca, the natives 'eat all the snakes, and lizards, and spiders, and worms that they find upon the ground', ahead of them were 'civilized people of intelligence'. This phrase occurs in the oath to which Columbus made all his men subscribe before turning back. It was clearly in the interest of Spain that contact with the civilized peoples of the East should be made, but it was not what Columbus wanted, and it was not what his weary seamen wanted. So they affirmed that Cuba was China and that it was pointless to go any further. Not all of them believed it, however. Juan de la Cosa, for instance, an experienced pilot and cartographer, signed the oath but showed Cuba as an island in his world map of 1500. But if it is more accurate to see Columbus as a prospector than as a disinterested explorer, he rounded out men's knowledge of the West Indies on this voyage by discovering Dominica, the Leeward and Guadalupe Islands, Puerto Rico and Jamaica and by revealing more about both the coast and the interior of Hispaniola (Haiti and Santo Domingo).

The third voyage, though conducted in the same spirit, led to an even more important discovery: the north coast of South America. There is no evidence that Columbus' instructions were other than to take his six ships out to Hispaniola, where the early colonists were in need of supplies. He split the fleet *en route*, however, and took three of them further south than he had sailed before, to the Cape Verde islands, and only then turned west. In his administrative capacity he had made serious blunders. Complaints of his high-handedness and lack of judgement had streamed back to Spain. He needed wealth, gold, more than ever, both for himself and to impress the Catholic Monarchs. So, for two reasons, he went south. He had received a letter from a cosmographically-minded expert in gems who had heard from 'many Indians and Arabs and Ethiopians that the majority of precious things come from a very hot region' – and Columbus noted in his journal that he set his course because 'more gold and things of value' are found in southern latitudes. His second reason was to verify the rumours, coming mainly from Portugal, about the existence of land to the south-west – the rumours that had prompted John II to contest the ruling of *Inter Caetera*. Such a land, being marked on no maps, would presumably not be part of the organized Cathayan realms but open to exploitation.

And he found it; homing in along the tenth parallel he discovered Trinidad and, to the south again, the delta of the Orinoco. His first instinct was to believe this to be another island, but forcing his ships against the great current of fresh water he realized that no island could feed so mighty a river. With this observation he wrote in his journal, 'I believe that this is a very great continent, which until today has been unknown'. This is straightforward cause and effect reasoning, but then he slips through any conventional sieve held out by historians to catch 'the Renaissance mind' and declares that the river flowed from the Earthly Paradise! This conclusion was based partly on observation, partly on his love of the poetry as well as the prose of exploration. Sailing repeatedly across the Atlantic, from watching his compass variation and stars he had become convinced that he was going uphill when going west, downhill when returning home. After leaving the Azores for the Antilles, 'the ships', he noted, 'went on rising smoothly towards the sky'. From east to west it became progressively warmer, and this was because his ships were being gently lifted towards the sun. He concluded that the earth was not round, as was commonly believed, but pearshaped, 'having a raised projection for the stalk, or like a woman's nipple on a round ball'. Thus for the prose. It was the poet's conviction that the Terrestrial Paradise 'is on the summit of the spot which I have described as being in the form of the stalk of a pear . . . and if the water of which I speak does not proceed from the Earthly Paradise, it appears to be still more marvellous, for I do not believe that there is any river in the world so large or so deep'. Columbus had to take his rotting stores to Hispaniola after reaching this conclusion, leaving the exploration of Paradise to the less mystical Conquistadores.

Affairs in Hispaniola were in such administrative chaos, and he was the object of so much loathing that his return to Spain was made in another man's ship, and in chains. It was not until 1502 that his pleas to be allowed a further voyage were granted by the Catholic Kings. By this time the coast of South America had been patchily explored from well down the Brazilian coast to the Isthmus of Panama. Belief that all this land was part of Asia was fading. If it was, however, there was one last chance of proving it, by finding a strait between the 'new' continent and the Golden Chersonese that would lead to India – the India which Portugal was now in regular contact with via the Cape. All the maps showed that it was possible to circumnavigate the Chersonese peninsula, and Marco Polo had actually done so in a Chinese vessel. Cuba had now been revealed as an island so this time Columbus sailed further west, making land at Puerto Castilla, half-way along the north shore of Honduras. And here, instead of turning west, which would have brought him into touch with the Mayan civilization of Yucatan he turned east, clawing along the coast of Honduras in the teeth of constant gales. Possibly he was influenced by the north-westerly set of the Gulf Stream, possibly by a glimpse of the well-organized trading world he had always fought shy of. For soon after his arrival in Honduras the Spaniards met a large canoe coming from the west with a cargo of artefacts more sophisticated than any they had yet seen in the Caribbean: coloured cottons, copper hatchets and bells, ceramic wares and objects carved from obsidian and onyx.

Rounding Honduras he came south along the shores of Nicaragua and Costa Rica to the Darien coast of Panama. Then, at the entrance to the modern Panama Canal, ill, and in charge of leaking ships, Columbus turned back to Jamaica. The Indians had made it clear that this was an isthmus, with another ocean beyond it. But to Columbus, shipwrecked on Jamaica, ill and crazed by disappointment and privation, it was still mainland and he had been, as he explained in a weird and rambling letter to his sovereigns, within ten days march of the river Ganges – within reach of mountains of gold. Gold, he explained in this tragic mixture of the bible, geographical theory and folk-lore, 'gold is the most precious of all commodities; gold constitutes treasure, and he who possesses it has all he needs in this world, as also the means of rescuing souls from purgatory, and restoring them to the enjoyment of paradise'. Columbus was rescued after a full year and died in 1504, shortly after his return to Spain. Whether, in the last bitter years, he changed his mind about the nature of Central America is unknown. But the Zorzi sketch maps, drawn about 1509 from information derived from his brother Bartholemew who had been his second-in-command on the voyage of 1502-3, convey no doubt: scrawled across the hinterland of Nicaragua is the uncompromising word *ASIA*.

If I have concentrated on Columbus it is because his discoveries of the Antilles, the north coast of South America and that of Central America were the crucial ones, and because the Columbian documents allow us to see the confusion through which the explorers groped towards an understanding of a new world. Columbus' original picture of the world was burned too deep into his imagination to allow its revision in the light of what he found; most likely he died, the Savonarola of exploration, still believing in his visions. But his discoveries allowed other men to assemble the real picture with a speed they owed to him. In 1501 Amerigo Vespucci, who had already sailed east from the mouth of the Orinoco to the tip of Brazil, was sent to follow up Cabral's isolated landing, and coasted far to the south; on a subsequent voyage it is possible – the evidence is unclear – that he explored as far as Patagonia. Vespucci was not an inspired seaman, he was a geographer. He never commanded an expedition of his own but was sent as a man specially trained in the interpretation of discoveries. It was by grafting his accounts of the vast length of the South American shore on to Columbus' failure to find a strait through Central America that the German geographer Martin Waldseemüller published a world map in 1507 that showed all the sightings reported from the west, from Labrador to the Argentine, as one continent. He called it, from Vespucci's Christian name, America. Waldseemüller showed, too, another ocean between America and Asia, but his example was not generally followed until Vasco Nuñez de Balboa, taking up where Columbus had left off on his fourth voyage and, like him, thirsting for gold, crossed the Isthmus of Panama and, in 1513, saw the Pacific. The spectral Asia had been banished. The problem now was to get to the real one past the American barricade.

In 1519 Ferdinand Magellan left from Spain to show how it could be done by sailing round South America, but the length of this voyage, the ghastly suffering from scurvy and starvation (the crews ate rats and leather from the rigging in the Pacific) and its dangers (Magellan was killed by natives in the Philippines and the circumnavigation was completed by one ship out of five), these factors dissuaded others from following. A voyage of three years, thirty-five survivors out of two hundred and eighty; it is not surprising that Magellan's feat was not repeated until 1577, when Francis Drake left Plymouth on a voyage that also took nearly three years. The exploration of the east coast of South America was left to the Conquistadores, searching for gold and silver in Peru and Chile, and the speed with which this was done may be seen by comparing the superb world map of Diogo Ribeiro (1527), in which the east coast is entirely blank, with Mercators' world map of 1538 which gives an accurate coastline for Colombia, Ecuador and Peru, and then labels the coast further to the south 'Littora Incognita'. By 1562, maps were giving the whole outline of South America with confidence, though most showed the southern shore of Magellan's Straits as part of the huge circumpolar continent 'Terra Australis'.

Memories of Asia lingered on after Columbus' death in the far north, where John Cabot had reached what he thought to be Cathay. The Caribbean and South America were clearly new lands, but it is only justice to Columbus' memory to stress with what stubbornness men stretched Asia towards Europe in the north, conveying the Bering Straits to the waters between Labrador and Greenland.

This was only possible while there was a gap in their knowledge between Newfoundland and the Columban area. This was filled by Giovanni da Verrazano who sailed from France in 1523 to Florida (discovered by Ponce de Leon in 1513, but believed to be an island) and coasted north. His aim is revealing. 'My intention in this navigation was to reach Cathay and the extreme east of Asia, not expecting to find such an obstacle of new land as I found; and if for some reason I expected to find it, I thought it not to be without some strait to penetrate to the Eastern Ocean. And this has been the opinion of all the ancients, believing certainly our Western Ocean to be one with the Eastern Ocean of India without interposition of land.' His progress up the Carolina coast to New York and up as far as Cape Breton, where, his stores exhausted, he turned for home, disillusioned him and established that from the Straits of Magellan to Nova Scotia, America was one continent, but he was still influenced by the magic of Cathay into making one great error. Missing the entrance to Chesapeake Bay between Cape Henry and Cape Charles, but seeing its broad waters across the arm of Eastern Maryland farther north, he concluded that this was no mere strait but the

Eastern Ocean itself, mysteriously barred from contact with the Western Ocean. For some sixty years many North American maps were to show a gigantic watery wedge nearly splitting North America in two.

This power of legend was not only felt in the north. Men were drawn into Mexico and Peru not only by the wealth that was actually there, but by legends of still greater wealth that was always a little further on. The exploration of the Gulf of Mexico and the southern United States from Florida to the Grand Canyon was motivated by a search for a mystical Fountain of Youth that could make an old man lusty again, and by rumours of the Empire of Cibola with its seven cities of gold. When Peru had fallen there was still the Empire of El Dorado, the Golden Man, to find.

In Peru, there were gold objects but no mines. These were assumed to be now further south, now further east, and expedition after expedition (sometimes fostered by cynical governors of Peru, glad to be rid of the more rowdy of the settlers) hacked their way through the hinterlands of Colombia, Venezuela and Guiana. El Dorado proved as elusive as Prester John was to prove in Africa, but as his gilded will-o'-the-wisp was heard of here and confidently reported there, the map of South America, its mountain ranges and its rivers, emerged as men pursued him. The same was true in North America; the Indian kingdoms Cartier failed to find still acted as a lure – as late as 1634, Nicollet was led to Lake Superior by descriptions of Indians west of the St. Lawrence who sounded to him like Japanese. Such legends, and the still glimmering phantom of Cathay which kept men searching both the east and west coasts of North America for a route there more practical than Verrazano's sea: these factors, as much as furs and silver and dyewoods, and much more than disinterested geographical curiosity, influenced the emergence of the Americas from the void. In their pursuit of visions, no less than in their iron determination and practical skills, the followers of Columbus were indeed his heirs.

4
Far North and Far South

By the middle of the sixteenth century, as a result of voyages east and west, a broad belt of the world between roughly 40° north and 40° south was known and mapped in a way we would accept as realistic. The Pacific islands (which lie mostly between 10° north and 30° south) were missing, because Magellan's Pyrrhic victory had shown that his triumph was not worth copying for trade purposes. The west coast of North America was still a guess – California, for instance, was commonly believed to be an island. The East Indies varied from map to map because the Portuguese and Spaniards did not voluntarily pass on information to one another or to other nations, but were a composite map to have been made up, it would have been fairly accurate except for the south coast of New Guinea and the whole region below 10° south.

The most accurately defined areas, the Caribbean, Central and South America to 20° south, and Africa, Arabia, India, Malaysia and Indonesia, represent the Spanish and Portuguese trading areas. These were not only the best known, but the easiest zones to represent on maps, for as degrees of longitude narrowed in approaching the poles landmarks became harder and harder to plot; one of the chief causes of the sensational advance in geographical knowledge between Columbus' first voyage and Magellan's circumnavigation was that exploring activity had centred on the equator, where the Moluccas lay. And the position of Cathay and the Spice Islands – the Moluccas are 140° east of Lisbon – drew ships towards them round both sides of the world. Had gold and spices been found in the mid-

Atlantic, the exploration of the whole sub-tropical belt would probably have been indefinitely postponed.

The position of the Moluccas is, then, the key to the first century of exploration. It is also the key to most of the coastal exploration of the second, for when other nations, the French, the English and the Dutch, entered the search for overseas trade in earnest, it was still Cathay and the Spice Islands that were the goal. But new routes had to be found. The sub-tropical lanes were patrolled by the Iberian powers: Spain via Mexico to the Philippines, Portugal via Africa and the Indian Ocean. As early as five years after the survivors of Magellan's circumnavigation returned, the English merchant Robert Thorne drew the obvious conclusion. 'There is but one way to discover,' he wrote to Henry VIII, 'which is to the North . . . For out of Spain they have discovered all the Indies and seas occidental, and out of Portugal all the Indies and seas oriental, so that by this part of the orient and occident they have compassed the world.' In typical Renaissance style he takes an aggressive patriotism for granted, for 'experience proveth that naturally all princes be desirous to extend and enlarge their dominions', and he proceeds on the assumption that Henry will want to break into the spice zone by finding northern routes round Asia or America.

He was right. In that same year Henry VIII sent two ships, the *Mary of Guildford* and the *Samson*, to search for a north-west passage. Their failure to get further than Labrador because of the ice showed that the project would be difficult, but the fact that one of the vessels, turning south into the Caribbean (possibly to test the chances of interloping) was nearly captured by the Spanish, confirmed Thorne's diagnosis of the need for northern routes.

The search for north-west or north-east passages that followed is the most bizarre episode in the history of exploration. Bizarre because, unlike the attempts to circumnavigate Africa and America by the south, it was totally impracticable given the vessels and the navigational techniques of the time. Indeed, it was not until 326 years after Frobisher's attempt to find a north-east passage that in 1879 Baron Nordenskjöld rounded northern Asia, and that was in a specially equipped steamer. It was not until 1906 that Amundsen's *Gjöa* fulfilled Thorne's vision, and this was after generations of expert surveying from both sides of northern Canada by ice-break-ers and sled parties. The existence of icebergs and pack ice was known not only from explorers like Sebastian Cabot whose crews, in 1509, mutinied and forced him to turn back at the mouth of Hudson Bay, but to the scores of fishing vessels from the Atlantic coast which went to the Newfoundland banks for cod. Of the two ships which made the first attempt to find a north-east passage in 1553, one was trapped in the ice and remained there till its com-mander, Sir Hugh Willoughby, and all his crew were dead.

Yet in spite of this knowledge, and of one fruitless or fatal voyage after another, the expeditions still sailed on their impossible mis-sions. The difficulties were not only physical – and it should be remembered that scurvy was as much a killer in the north as in the tropics – but also sprang from the inability of one explorer to pass on his knowledge to another. It was not only that in high latitudes it was almost impossible to correlate a dead-reckoning estimate of distance with the actual size of the arc travelled, but in the region of the magnetic pole the compass was subject to extremes of variation. The outlines traced on a chart might be clear enough, but when this information came to be incorporated in a map covering a larger area, it might well be fitted into the wrong place in the jigsaw of straits, fjords and islands. Time after time the same mistakes were made, the same opportunities missed. But in spite of this the search persisted. In the face of mounting evidence to the contrary there were men in each succeeding generation who blithely echoed Thorne's opinion that the northern route, eastwards or westwards, 'may so easily and with so little cost, labour and danger be followed'.

This persistence arose from the magnitude of the prize to be gained, by a stubborn belief in the gold of Cathay and the undoubted evidence of the spice-scented quays of Lisbon and Seville. And it was backed by a conviction, based on geographical theory, that the northern routes did exist and, given a little extra determination and luck, could be found. Thorne believed, as had Columbus, that the most valuable products were to be found where the sun's rays were most direct, and where the Iberians now swaggered and prospered. 'As our metals be lead, tin and iron, so theirs be gold, silver and copper. And as our fruits and graines be apples, nuts and corn, so theirs be dates, nutmegs, pepper, cloves and other spices.' The message of patriotism and profit was clear, and, geographically, there was no bar, for, apart from 'two or three leagues' of dangerous waters when rounding each side of the northernmost capes of Africa and Asia, thereafter all was open water and plain sailing; by east or west, the ships would slope easily down to the coasts of Cathay. What is more, the polar routes would be some two thousand leagues shorter than those used by the Spaniards and Portuguese. And as for those who feared that to cross the Arctic circle would be as fatal as crossing the equator had once been feared to be, Thorne dismissed them with the comment that 'there is no land uninhabitable nor sea unnavigable'.

I have quoted Thorne's views at some length because although there was a constant and lively interest in geographical theory in Renaissance England among scholars and merchants and some of the better educated gentry, there was little development from Thorne's ideas. Over and over again his last remark was paraphrased as a reason to take up the weary fight once again; God had created the world for man, so the polar regions must be habitable. As George Best, who had accompanied Frobisher on three abortive searches for the north-west passage, put it with dogged faith: 'I cannot think that the divine providence hath made anything uncommunicable' – therefore it must be possible to sail from London to Cathay past the pole. And though Cartier, in a moment of exasperation, called the Labrador coast 'the land that God gave Cain', meetings with Eskimoes in the west and Samoyeds in the east gave support to the 'no land uninhabitable' form of encouragement. And Thorne's belief that once the northern capes had been rounded the coast would trend south into the Pacific after a few tough days was restated in 1580 by no less a man than the great cartographer, Mercator. 'The voyage to Cathay by the east,' he wrote, 'is doubtless very easy and short, and I have oftentimes marvelled that being so happily begun it hath been left off.' In that year, indeed, Arthur Pet and Richard Jackman were sent off to try again, and few documents convey better the benign confidence of the armchair experts than the instructions penned for them by Richard Hakluyt and the mathematician-cosmographer, John Dee.

Along the Asian coast they would find the coast climbing north-wards to Cape Tabin (for which the authority was Pliny, who had never been farther north than the Roman *limes*) after turning which they would coast south-east and could either enter Cathay by 'the famous river Oechardes' (a myth) or carry on and circumnavigate the eastern tip of Asia by the Strait of Anian (another myth, supported by its existence on maps until Vitus Bering's conjecture was confirmed by Captain Cook), through which they would pass to the Chinese coast. They were to take note, while the weather was still cold, of whether the coast were populous or no. If it were, then this would be an obvious outlet for warm English woollen cloth. If it were not, then they should count the whales and look out for fish, as this might be an excellent substitute for the Newfoundland Banks and the waters off Iceland. And if the air were mild and land fruitful, 'then we may plant on that main the offals of our people' – those beggars and sturdy vagabonds that were such a bugbear to the Elizabethans. On arrival at their destination they were to take samples of seeds, to dry fruits and herbs and to study the customs of the natives, especially what they wore, how they fought and what goods they lacked. To convince the suave Chinese that the English, though rough mariners, came from a civilized country, they were to take 'boxes with weights for gold . . . to show that the people here use weight and measure, which is a certain show of wisdom and of certain government settled here'. And they were also to take 'all the general silver coins of our English monies . . . which is a thing that shall in silence speak to wise men more than you imagine'. They were also to be sure to perfume the ship before the Chinese come aboard, and to give them olives with their wine, and present them with marmalade and make sure they studied a map of London with the river 'full of ships'.

Pet and Jackman had no chance to present their Latin letters from Queen Elizabeth (they were thoughtfully provided with translations) to Cathayan princes, or to estimate the market for anti-dust spectacles on the Chinese plains. Fighting the ice, they reached the Kara sea before they were squeezed out by the expanding packs of autumn. Pet got back to London through freezing storms, his crew scarcely able to man the ship from exposure. Jackman went down with all hands off the coast of Norway.

With the failure of this mission, English interest in the north-east passage slackened. Something had been gained, both for trade and for geographical knowledge. Though Willoughby had perished in 1533, his second-in-command, Richard Chancellor, had gained Archangel in the White Sea and opened up an overland route from there to Moscow which was exploited by the Muscovy Company, formed in London in 1554. And before the two ships became separated they had reached Novaya Zemlya. Three years later Stephen Burrough, with a crew of eight in the tiny *Searchthrift*, became the first explorer to pass through the southern strait between Novaya Zemlya and Vaigach Island and enter the Kara Sea. But here the advance stopped, and Pet and Jackman, though briefed by Burrough, could get no farther than this frozen wilderness.

The next explorers to tackle the ice of the Kara Sea were Dutch. In two expeditions, in 1594 and 1595, Willem Barents explored the whole of the west coast of Novaya Zemlya and forced his way as far as the mouth of the Ob. But his greatest achievement was a voyage made in the following year. This time he gave the North Cape of Norway a wide berth and discovered Bear Island – named after a two hour battle with a polar bear – and, still further north, the jagged peaks of Spitzbergen, which he took to be part of the east coast of Greenland. Turning east he rounded the northern point of Novaya Zemlya only to find himself pinned by the ice and forced to winter in a bay, Ice Haven, a little way down the east coast. In spring, unable to work the vessel free, Barents and his men set off for home in open boats; weak and ill, it was not many days before Barents died. When Ice Haven was next visited, in 1871, among the relics found there was a letter from Barents explaining how the ice was holding up his search for Cathay.

The Ob remained the farthest point reached by sea before the days of iron hulls and propellers. The residual warmth of the north Atlantic current dies away west of Novaya Zemlya and beyond lies a chancy battle with floe and pack ice. The exploration of northern Asia went forward in the seventeenth century but – as was the case in Canada in the same period – it was the work of fur-trappers and those semi-merchants, semi-bandits who were the land equivalent of the maritime privateers. Such men reached Lake Baikal in the south, and by 1618 reached the outlet of the Lena in the Laptev Sea. In 1647 part of the aim of those who sought a north-east passage was accomplished when a party of Cossacks left the mouth of the Kolyma and became the first men to sail round the north-east promontory of Asia and, crossing the Gulf of Anadyr, to reach northern Kamchatka.

Baffled in the north-east, the geographers and merchants turned to the north-west, the other route represented by Thorne to give easy access to Cathay. In this direction there were alternative theories. One balanced the north-eastern view by seeing the problem in terms of getting far enough north to be able to round the north-east corner of America, after which it was merely a matter of coasting south-west down to the Pacific via the Strait of Anian. Another saw an enormous extension of eastern Asia reaching into the North Atlantic, with America, as it were, under the shelter of its arm and separated by a strait (John Dee thought the St. Lawrence to be such a strait) which would lead directly to Cathay. Thirdly, Verrazano's Sea still plagued certain maps with its promise of a wasp waist bringing the Pacific to within a few miles of the coast of Virginia. Of these theories the first, which is indeed the nearest to the truth, was the most popular. And it was all the more so because, just as in the north-east passage theories it was thought that a great river might be found leading to the heart of Cathay before the Strait of Anian was reached, it was believed by many that soon after rounding north-east America a strait would be found running into the Pacific well east of Anian itself. These hopeful dreams were not in fact dispelled until Samuel Herne's exploration of the Coppermine, and Alexander Mackenzie's of the Mackenzie River (1770 and 1789), had shown that they were not crossed by any strait, and until Vancouver's coastal survey of British Columbia and the Yukon (1791–5) had proved that there was no outlet from the Arctic into the Pacific east of Bering Strait.

The failure of Willoughby and Burrough having led to a temporary discouragement among the proponents of the north-east passage, Sir Humphrey Gilbert took advantage of this mood to write what was to be a very influential work, his *Discourse for a Discovery for a new Passage to Cathay*. In this he argued strongly for the north-west route as the easier; he pictured indeed a northern coastline for America that ran from Hudson's Strait to Seattle. Once more we are in that familiar Renaissance atmosphere where the evidence of the eye and of ancient authorities commingle as equals. Pliny had recorded the arrival of 'Indians' in Europe. They could not have come from the south, their crafts were too frail, the distance too far, the winds too contrary. They could not have come via the north-east – witness the ice barriers found by English seamen. So they must have come via a north-west passage. And this passage led straight from the Pacific. There were those who argued that Asia and America were joined together in northern latitudes. Impossible. Was not America the continent Plato had described as Atlantis? The ancients had thought it nearer Europe than America had turned out to be, but their critics forgot that there had been great floods and earthquakes which had drowned its eastern parts, leaving only the present continent as dry land. These same floods had made the north-west passage even broader than it was before. Moreover, if America were not an island, why had no Asiatic peoples or animals been found there? It is true that no-one can now be found who has seen the north-west passage with his own eyes, but 'the diversity between brute beasts and men, or between the wise and the simple, is that the one judgeth by sense only and gathereth no surety of anything that he hath not seen, felt, heard, tasted or smelled, and the other not so only, but also findeth the certainty of things by reason, before they happen to be tried'.

To the historian of ideas, this defence of the power of the human mind is moving in one way, to the historian of events in another; he sees the vision of the mind's eye tested in a series of ghastly encounters with reality. The names of those who were chosen to verify Gilbert's reasoning, Frobisher, Davis, Hudson, Baffin and Foxe, have all gained the immortality of the gazetteer; their names are attached to bays, straits and inlets, but none succeeded, all suffered, and one (Hudson) died. And all lost many, and some lost most, of their crews. Knowledge was, of course, gained. By the middle of the seventeenth century the relationship of Greenland to Baffin Island was reasonably clear, the coast of Labrador and the nature of Hudson Bay and Hudson Strait were established. But this, until stronger ships and improved medical and navigational techniques were available, was knowledge as barren as the area itself. The major contribution of these men was to prevent future generations from sacrificing lives in a search for a trade route that did not exist.

The contradiction must not be sentimentalized. There was no clear distinction between those who theorized and those who were deputed to test the theories. Frobisher thought that he had found the entrance to the passage (his 'strait' had to be altered to Frobisher's Bay) in 1576; Davis had to turn back in 1587 from the ice at the head of Baffin Bay but he could still write that 'the passage is most probable, the execution easy'. And Gilbert himself died at sea on the return voyage from his planting of the first British colony in America. 'North of the Azores', wrote a mariner in his sister ship, 'the frigate was near cast away, oppressed by waves, yet at that time recovered. And giving forth signs of joy, the general, sitting aloft with a book in his hand, cried out to us in the *Hind*, so oft as we did approach within hearing,"we are as near to heaven by sea as by land"'. That night' (so this, one of the most famous passages in Hakluyt's *Voyages*, continues) 'the frigate being ahead of us in the *Golden Hind*, suddenly her lights were out . . . for in that moment the frigate was devoured and swallowed up of the sea'.

And though it is above all in the pages of Hakluyt that the rigours of this phase of polar exploration can be re-experienced most vividly, and though it was for the most part English seamen who fended their way through the ice of Hudson Bay, belief in a northwest passage claimed other victims. In 1619, for instance, the Norwegian merchant-mariner Jens Munk sailed from Copenhagen for Hudson Bay with sixty-five men. He returned next year with three. The others died about him as his ship lay in the ice in Button Bay – named for Thomas Button, who had explored the western shore of Hudson Bay in 1612–3. When spring came with a few faint warm airs, Munk, too weak to move away from the stench that began to arise from his dead shipmates, wrote painfully in his journal: 'Inasmuch as I have now no more hope of life in this world, I request, for the sake of God, if any Christian men should happen to come here, that they will bury in the earth my poor body, together with the others which are found here, expecting their reward from God in Heaven . . . therewith, good-night to all the world; and my soul into the hand of God.' But the spring also brought with it a little grass. The three men sucked its roots and became strong enough to fish and at last to shoot birds. Pitching the bodies overboard they pushed the *Lamprey* out through the melting ice and brought her battered and leaking through the strait, past Greenland and back to Norway.

By the middle of the seventeenth century the northern passages were recognized for what they were: myths congealed in the ice of Hudson Bay and the Kara Sea. The southern myth, the myth of Terra Australis, was more obstinate, and its demise only took place long after the limits of this book, with Cook's voyage in the *Resolution* in 1772–5.

The conception of a huge southern land mass owed its inception to the dislike of the Renaissance for empty oceanic spaces on maps: if an area of the globe were unknown, then the *horror vacui* instinct filled it not with *Mare* but with *Terra Incognita*. This instinct was confirmed by a theory that the world would topple over if there were not enough weight of land in the southern hemisphere to balance Europe and Asia. And as the work of exploration proceeded Terra Australis became even more necessary as a repository for the legendary lands that could not be found in Africa and Asia, for Marco Polo's gold-bearing kingdom of Locac and Pentam, his island of spices, and for Solomon's Ophir. As maps increasingly refined the true outline of Africa, Asia and the Americas they gave at the same time an increasingly impressive bulk and precision to the as yet undiscovered southern continent. It filled the seas as far as Capricorn – and even farther north: when the north coast of New Guinea was found in 1528 it was at once hailed as a promontory of Terra Australis, bringing part of the southern continent almost up to the equator.

On Mercator's influential world map of 1569, Magellan's Strait leads directly into Terra Australis, whose coast climbs steadily thence across the South Atlantic and, after a southerly dip between 65° and 90° east, sweeps up again to 15° south before sloping across the

Pacific to incorporate Tierra del Fuego. When Tierra del Fuego's island status was confirmed by voyages like that of Drake (1578), Terra Australis was grudgingly pushed back – at that point; when Hawkins came upon the Falkland Islands a few years later, though they are near Tierra del Fuego and more northerly, he took them without question to be part of Terra Australis. Well after Java had been circumnavigated maps continued to represent it as a promontory of the southern continent. Its existence was an obsession for every voyager in the southern regions of the Atlantic, the Pacific or the Indian Ocean. When the Spanish explorer Quiros, for example, arrived at one of the New Hebrides islands (15° south) in 1606, he was convinced that he had achieved his aim of discovering Terra Australis. Australia was assumed to be part of the southern continent until Tasman sailed below it in 1642, but though he pushed back the limits of Terra Australis there he thought he had found it again when he came upon the west coast of New Zealand. The only 'real' southern continent is, of course, Antarctica, but it was centuries before it was sliced back, voyage by voyage, and finally dissolved into the island groups and the polar continent of our modern maps.

This urge to expect land where there was none, which led Pacific voyagers to see fog banks as Australasian capes or patches of dead calm as the drowned reefs of Ophir, reveals more about the mentality of Renaissance man than mere greed for gold, or the desire to bring new peoples to Christ or the conservatism of cosmographers. It reflects, of course, a justifiable fear; fear of running short of food, fear of the diseases, especially scurvy, which haunted every long voyage without landfalls. But it also reflects a sociability, an appetite for things, for contacts. There is nothing in the sources for the history of exploration that anticipates the modern love of drifting for drifting's sake, or the voluntary suspension for long periods of commitment to people or places. No men of the Renaissance had 'individualism' forced on them more strongly by circumstance than the explorers, yet no men show more clearly the uneasiness men felt when isolated from the neighbourliness, the community feeling that has been seen as a characteristic of the medieval as opposed to the Renaissance world. It was in no mood of casual detachment, of self-sufficiency, that the explorers sailed the empty tracts that we look on as recuperative pauses for self-reassurance; they sailed to clearly imagined goals and, when these turned out to be in fact imaginary, compensated for their disappointment and alarm by saying that they had at least been near the shores of Locac or Pentam. There is a psychological, as well as a cosmographical, explanation for the persistent belief in a southern continent of gigantic dimensions.

In addition, the impossibility of recording longitude accurately before the marine chronometer came into use in the eighteenth century made it difficult to plot the Pacific islands, and easy to see a landfall as part of Terra Australis though it had already been identified as an island by an earlier voyager. The Spaniard Mendaña discovered the Solomons in 1568, naming them for the riches of the province of Ophir, which he assumed must be not far away. Then they were lost again – Mendaña himself searching unsuccessfully in a later voyage. Later they were several times rediscovered and given new names, and it was not until two centuries had passed that Cook recognized them and restored the name they had been given by Mendaña.

In fact, however, few islands were discovered before the middle of the seventeenth century. The physical hazards of a trans-Pacific voyage were made clear by the losses incurred. Only one ship survived from Magellan's fleet. Several early attempts by Spaniards to cross from Mexico ended in disaster, and it was not until 1565 that a ship, Alonso de Arellano's *San Lucas*, crossed the Pacific in the reverse direction, from the Philippines. Moreover, the Pacific, by Tordesillas and the logic of her trade interest, was a Spanish zone, and the wind patterns made it impossible to explore the south Pacific by sailing westwards from South America; the south-east trades lifted ships steadily up towards the equator, leaving the chief island groups of Polynesia and Melanesia south of their involuntary course. The most that could be achieved was to make contact with the northern parts of Terra Australis that were shown looming up towards Indonesia.

In 1567 Alvaro de Mendana set off with two ships from Peru to find and to settle a colony in the mythical southern continent; we have seen that he reached the Solomons, but he got no further south than 11°. Sir Francis Drake entered the Pacific through the Straits of Magellan in 1578, but his original orders, which were to look for Terra Australis, had been changed to a privateering expedition up the coasts of Chile and Peru, and while he noted that he could not see the southern continent as he entered the Pacific, he was not concerned to challenge seriously the assertions of his maps. In 1595 Mendaña made a second voyage, coming upon several islands in the Marquesas and Santa Cruz groups but again not getting farther south than 11°. Even Pedro Fernandez de Quiros, who had gained invaluable experience as Mendaña's chief pilot, and who made in 1606 a determined attempt to strike south, was unable to get further than 24° (in which latitude he discovered the Tuamotu group) before he was carried up north of the Fiji's to the northern New Hebrides where, in a bay on Espiritu Santo island, he devoutly took possession for Philip III of 'all this region of the south as far as the pole, which from this time shall be called' – not Terra Australis, simply, but – 'Australia del Espiritu Santo, with all its dependencies for ever and so long as right exists'. A month later, after attempting to found a town named the New Jerusalem on a river he dubbed the Jordon, he set out to find more of the southern continent but was forced, by storms and the reluctance of his men, to cross the equator and return to Mexico.

His conviction that he had been almost within sight of the mainland of Terra Australis gave cartographers greater confidence than ever in its existence. The legend did receive a minor blow as a result of this expedition however; Quiros' second-in-command, Luis Vaez de Torres, continued to the west, and by passing south of New Guinea through the strait which bears his name today proved that the imagined mainland did not rise up, at least to within two degrees of the equator. But it was not until the Dutch, early in the seventeenth century, began to investigate the seas south of Indonesia by striking down from their possessions in Java that Australia was discovered and, in 1642, lopped away from Terra Australis by Tasman; and it was not until Cook entered the Pacific from the west that the winds enabled him to keep so close to the Antarctic Circle that Terra Australis was, with some reluctance, removed finally from maps and charts, the legend at last cut down to size.

5
Men and Methods

The explorer's ship was small. Columbus' *Nina* was 60 tons, Drake's *Pelican* (re-named en route the *Golden Hind*) about 120, and his companion ships, the *Elizabeth* and the *Marigold* were 80 and 30 tons respectively. Frobisher discovered the bay named after him in the *Gabriel*, of 50 tons, and Davis' remarkable voyage to find a north-west passage was made with the 50 ton *Sunshine* and the *Moonshine* of 35 tons. The ships were small for three reasons: to cut down the investment in a project whose profits were conjectural; to ensure a reasonable speed (about seven knots in a fair wind) so that provisions would hold out between landfalls; and because their purpose was to explore coastlines, and this involved sailing over shoals and up narrow creeks. We would not be far wrong in thinking of 50–60 tons as an average size.

Even then this size represented a compromise between the weatherliness required for oceanic voyages and the shallow draft needed for coastal exploration. So, commonly, the explorers took a pinnace with them, either secured across the ship's well or stored in pieces for assembly on the spot. Da Gama carried such a pinnace-kit with him, which he left on station duty off Mocambique. Drake took four pinnaces in pieces and Frobisher had two on his voyage in 1577. Little use was made of indigenous small craft; Cartier's use of Indian canoes on the rivers of eastern Canada was exceptional. Europeans preferred to carry or build boats like their own than to trusting dug-out or birch-bark.

The crew of a 50–60 ton ship would be in the neighbourhood of twenty-five men. This proportion of crew to size had an important effect on the conduct of a voyage of exploration. One of the major problems was that of food supply. Before the handling of sails became easier thanks to the improvements in rigging that developed during the seventeenth century, a ship needed a large number of hands in relation to its size. Lack of refrigeration, the bad keeping qualities even of salt meat and salt fish, the propensity of grain and biscuit to become sour or weevilly, the shortage of storage space for liquids and the propensity of the best made casks (which they seldom were) to spring a leak with the continual lurching of the ship: all these were factors that modified a voyager's ability to sail where he chose. In heading from the South Atlantic for the Pacific, for instance, rather than give a treacherous coast a wide berth and sail round Cape Horn, he would face the hazards of Magellan's Strait in order to salt penguins for the next leg of his journey. And the fact that ships could not at that date sail close to the wind meant that far more laborious tacking was needed than is the case with sail today. This also increased the strain on food supplies, and induced an island-hopping mentality wherever there was a chance to indulge it.

The ship's company was a microcosm of society on land. A gentleman as captain, especially when the claiming of new territories or diplomacy with settled ones was in mind; a professional man, the pilot; a businessman (commonly, but not inevitably the master) who was usually the owner of the ship or his representative or an agent for the commissioning merchants; the officers and boatswain who were the equivalent of skilled artisans; and, most numerous, a proletariat of seamen, some of whom would be making the first voyage of their lives, and about half of whom would be boys: some members of Columbus' crew on his fourth voyage were twelve and thirteen. To make the analogy even more complete, some countries, especially Portugal, enrolled convicts who had been sentenced to death or banishment. Cabral took twenty among his fleet, da Gama ten or twelve. They were used as guinea-pigs to test the temper of possibly hostile natives, or were put ashore in the hope that if the ships had to put in there again they would find water and food: the castaways were given seeds, and sometimes chickens and goats to see if they could be domesticated. It was also hoped that they would learn the native language and – most hopeful of all – convert the local inhabitants to Christianity. Not surprisingly, the few records that have survived of rediscovered castaways show them all to have gone happily native.

It is about the common seamen that we know least. None has left an account of his motives or feelings; we can only guess about them. The chances of survival, taking the voyages of exploration as a whole, were about even. Danger, discomfort and privation were inevitable. And it is likely that only a small proportion of crews were seamen by training: one of the oddities of voyage narratives is the very rare mention of fishing even when supplies were dangerously short. They were illiterate, ignorant of – and therefore unfired by – geographical theory, and they were superstitious: Frobisher's men insisted on undressing an Eskimo woman to see if she were a witch or a devil. The folk-lore of geography, which would be the limit of their appreciation of a voyage's aims, stressed tempests, monsters and cannibals. It contained mountains of gold and rivers of precious stones as well, but these would be the perquisites of the captain and master.

In spite of this, no voyage failed to set out because crews could not be found, and some seamen even enlisted for a further voyage of exploration. There were mutinies, though only Henry Hudson died as the direct result of one, and very rarely a voyage could not be continued as far as the captain wanted because of this danger. But on the whole a supply of effective manpower could be taken for granted. Love of adventure, discontent with conditions at home: these motives can be taken for granted. The pay was not higher than for an ordinary trading voyage as a rule, but at least it was certain, for the backers, crown or merchant, were wealthy. The main complaint was not the danger, but the duration of a voyage. The married men especially missed their families – it was from experience of this that only bachelors were chosen for Barents' search for the north-east passage – and the long hauls produced a sense of exhausted pointlessness, movingly expressed by one of Quiros' seamen who complained to the pilot that 'he was tired of being always tired, that he would rather die once than many times, and that they might as well shut their eyes and let the ship go to the bottom'.

We must remember, moreover, that all seafaring was tough and dangerous in that age, and that life on land was hard and uncertain, pressing – for the sort of men who fled to sea – hard on the borders of subsistence; every flower and herb looked on not for its beauty but as a possible food or fertilizer. The average life expectation was thirty years. More farmers and tradesmen died of plague than did seamen of scurvy. So the hazards of exploration did not appear in such lurid contrast to ordinary life as they may appear to us; the crews were found, and the process of exploration was never without its human fuel.

We know hardly more about the pilots and ships' officers. They, too, could not expect to become rich; explorers did not sail looking for a fight at sea and prize money; the profits were taken by the backers. Only the soldiers, settlers and administrators who went out in the wake of the explorers might hope to make a fortune. The pilots, though skilled in getting a ship from one place to another were only very exceptionally learned enough to wish to go to sea in order to test the speculations of the landbound cosmographers. None, in our period, was able to master the advanced navigational techniques that astronomers and mathematicians had worked out for them. Again, we have to fall back on presumption: love of adventure, a guaranteed wage – with, sometimes, the possibility of a bonus; an inability to sense what we can see as the crucial distinction between a trading voyage and a voyage of exploration.

We are on firmer ground when we turn to the captains. But only relatively; men of action were at this time seldom introspective and though some of them described their own voyages and others found narrators, any description of motive or feeling is rare. But at least we can eke out the hints in these narratives with our knowledge of the class from which these highly literate, and usually well-born, leaders were drawn.

The desire for fame, to be remembered for great deeds, may with some confidence be included among their motives. And just as it was thought during the Renaissance that it was more glorious to fight conspicuously in a small skirmish than in the anonymous throng of a great army, so a man's name would ring out more clearly from unknown lands than from the hurly-burly competitiveness of Europe. It was written of Frobisher, when he set off to find the north-west passage, that 'he determined and resolved with himself to go and make full proof thereof, and to accomplish or bring back a certificate of the truth, or else never to return again, knowing this to be the only thing of the world that was left yet undone whereby a notable mind might be made famous and fortunate.'

Patriotism, the desire to do the state some service, can certainly be counted as an element in this desire for fame; exploration took on an air of national rivalry as soon as the West African voyages of the Portuguese began to show a profit.

Religious zeal, the desire to bring infidels to Christ, is less easy to pin down. Certainly religion permeated the process of exploration from the blessing of an expedition at its setting off, through ship-board services, to the thanksgiving on arrival. On Catholic voyages, at least, an effort was almost always made to tell the natives something of Christianity. Every mariner believed that he was to some extent in God's care, in almost every narrative there is a reference to some peril that would have overwhelmed the ship had it not been for God's mercy. For Catholics there was the special protection of the mariner's patron, St. Nicholas, and all seamen believed that when electricity glowed at the mast-head, St. Elmo was riding with them through the storm. For Catholics, again, the greatest number of place-names reflect the saint's day or church festival on which a landfall was made (though some of these have given way to more down-to-earth appellations: two harbourages named by Columbus in honour of the Conception of the Virgin have become Mosquito Bay and Rum Bay). But if explorers carried with them the consolation and encouragement that religion gave to cope with the perils of life as a whole, evangelical zeal was usually left for the professional missionaries who followed in their tracks. The explorers – Quiros being one of the few exceptions – were men of routine piety, but as collections of voyages came to be printed they could see themselves as the protagonists of a new cycle of romances in which reverberated some of the Christian feeling of the older romances of chivalry.

We can be more certain of curiosity, purposeful inquisitiveness, as a motive. In the pilgrim literature of the fifteenth century it is clear that curiosity was as great a factor in making men take the arduous journey to Palestine and Sinai as a longing to see the holy places. By 1502, the German humanist Konrad Celtis was complaining that his countrymen neglected to explore and describe their own countries, though they 'boasted of having travelled in Gaul and Spain, both Sarmathia and Pannonia, and even transoceanic countries'. It was curiosity as much as a search for some slaves who had been promised him that took Cadomosto into the interior of West Africa in 1455. 'My journey inland,' he wrote, 'was indeed more to see interesting sights and obtain information, than to receive my dues.' Pigafetta went with Magellan on his attempt to circumnavigate South America 'to experiment and go and see with my eyes a part of those things.' Ralph Fitch of London set off for the Spice Islands 'being desirous to see the countries of East India', and Pedro Teixeira, the first man to have gone round the world from west to east, said that though his achievement was partly the result of storms and other accidents, 'I was also inclined to it by curiosity.' But rather than multiply instances, I will quote the clearest account any Renaissance traveller left of his motives. It is from the memoirs of Ludovico Varthema, who sailed from Venice in 1502 on a journey that was to take him across Arabia to India and Malacca.

'There have been many men who have devoted themselves to the investigation of the things of this world, and by the aid of diverse studies, journeys, and very exact relations, have endeavoured to accomplish their desire. Others, again, of more perspicacious understandings, to whom the earth has not sufficed, such as the Chaldeans and Phoenicians, have begun to traverse the highest regions of Heaven with careful observations and watchings: from all which I know that each has gained most deserved and high praise from others and abundant satisfaction to themselves. Wherefore . . . I determined, personally, and with my own eyes, to endeavour to ascertain the situations of places, the qualities of peoples, the diversities of animals, the varieties of the fruit-bearing and odoriferous trees of Egypt, Syria, Arabia Deserta and Felix, Persia, India and Ethiopia, remembering well that the testimony of one eye-witness is worth more than ten heard-says.'

It is true that these quotations are taken mainly from freelance travellers, but if we do not find similar opinions in the narratives by or about the captains themselves, this is because the leader of an expedition had to subordinate his curiosity to a sense of purpose and responsibility. These narratives deal with the public, not the private aim, and with events, not opinions. It would be strange if the captains did not share the curiosity about new things that was shown so clearly by their sponsors, or were incapable of satisfying the thirst for information of the scholars and learned fellow-gentry who welcomed them home.

For the same reason the literature of exploration reveals very little about the nature of life at sea for the ship's company as a whole. Except for moments of special peril the voyage itself is taken for granted; the narrations concentrate on noting signs of hoped-for landfall, the nature of the land itself and the reception the seamen find there. There is commonly more *en route* detail in narratives of voyages in northern waters, but here again the emphasis is on hazards to navigation, ice and fog, rather than on the quality of life on board – let alone on the subjective impressions or reflections of the narrator. With Columbus as a notable exception, the mood of exploration is straightforwardly extrovert, the voyages accepted as a version of a normal trade voyage. The explorers did not watch themselves with the concern with which we watch them.

It may be, of course, that something of this impression of non-chalance comes from literary convention: the narratives are concerned with deeds, not with opinions. And a mood specific to the uncertainties of exploration was superimposed when, as frequently happened, the distance shown on the chart was covered and there was still no sign of land. The destinations were always known – at least they were thought to be known. The explorers had maps (ludicrously inaccurate, as we have seen) and they believed them. These led them to underestimate their difficulties. The amalgam of classical and medieval geographical theory had led map-makers to play up the amount of land on the earth's surface at the expense of the oceans and in these oceans they had inserted non-existent islands, and, in the case of Terra Australis, a non-existent continent. When we add the existence on maps of straits and passages that turned out to be imaginary we can see that the atmosphere of a voyage could turn quickly from one of normality to one of alarm – for almost always the unforeseen involved an extension of time, of food shortage and disease: weeks of unforeseen sailing: months of unforeseen incarceration in the ice. Storms, shipwreck, hostile inhabitants; these were hazards common to all seafaring, even in European waters. The dread novelty of exploration was delay: more explorers were martyrs to time than to typhoons, more were buried at sea than on the newly discovered shores.

With a minimum of fresh vegetables, with a diet potentially sound (3,500 calories a day has been estimated for a normal ship's diet) but always too salty and often putrid, living in stench, infested with fleas, lice and rats, seamen were natural victims of disease. Even when distances were known, as on the routine trading voyages between Lisbon and India, one death in five was expected. There was at least one case on the Manila-Acapulco route where a vessel was found drifting with every member of its crew dead. The importance of fresh fruit and vegetables was recognized – lime juice indeed was used on Lancaster's voyage to the east in 1601 – but lack of proper storage and disinfectants meant that scurvy could not be checked. The most graphic description of the disease – and its attempted cure – is given by a Frenchman, Jean Mocquet, who contracted it in the Indian Ocean.

'It rotted all my gums, which gave out a black and putrid blood. My knee joints were so swollen that I could not extend my muscles. My thighs and lower legs were black and gangrenous, and I was forced to use my knife each day to cut into the flesh in order to release this black and foul blood. I also used my knife on my gums, which were livid and growing over my teeth. I went on deck each day, and over to the bulwarks, clinging to the ropes, and holding a little mirror before me in my hand to see where it was necessary to cut. Then, when I had cut away this dead flesh and caused much black blood to flow, I rinsed my mouth and teeth with my urine, rubbing them very hard. But even with such treatment there was as much swelling of the gums again each day, and sometimes even more. And the unfortunate thing was that I could not eat, desiring more to swallow than to chew, because of my great suffering in this trying malady. Many of our people died of it every day, and we saw bodies being thrown into the sea constantly, three or four at a time. For the most part they died with no aid given them, expiring behind some case or chest, their eyes and the soles of their feet gnawed away by the rats.'

We know less about the lighter side of life on board. Some men read – Frobisher noted the consolation given by books – but apart from a story of Jesuit missionaries throwing chivalrous romances overboard and pressing tracts into the unwilling seamen's hands instead, we do not know what sort of reading matter was taken. The ship's musicians were doubtless employed to amuse the crew as well as to give signals. There is a moving description from a sister ship of how one of Sir Humphrey Gilbert's little fleet sailed through a fair Atlantic evening into the storm that drowned her, 'and most part of this Wednesday night, like the swan that singeth before her death, they in the *Delight* continued in sounding of trumpets, with drums and fifes, also winding the cornets and hautboys,' There are reference to sailors' and country dances, the performance of plays. By the late sixteenth century Crossing the Line was already marked by its usual horseplay. But the more usual anecdote to boredom was the forbidden gambling, a daily religious service and, on Catholic ships, the celebration of feast days with some semblance – weather and stores permitting – of an actual feast.

Voyages of exploration were organized by groups of merchants, with or without the co-operation of the crown, and these men consulted geographers and mathematicians before fixing the route to be taken. The leader of the expedition was given minute instructions of what to note as he sailed along. Those given in 1580 to Pet and Jackman were detailed and specific. They were told to chart new coast-lines with great care. 'When you come to have sight of any coast or land whatsoever, do you presently [at once] set the same with your sailing compass, how it bears off you, noting your judgement how far you think it from you, drawing also the form of it in your book, how it appears unto you, noting diligently how the highest or notablest part thereof beareth off you, and the extremes also in sight of the same land at both ends, distinguishing them by letter, A. B. C. etc.' They were to repeat such observations on different bearings, describing and drawing the landmarks – 'unto the which you may give apt names at your pleasure. The voyagers were also expected to compile vocabularies, so we have basic sixteenth century word lists in Malayalam and Patagonian, and know that the Eskimo for 'kiss me' was 'cany glow'.

Instructions to the pilot insisted that he took regular sun and star sights (infrequently complied with), noted the day's run and any unusual phenomena – weed patches, strong currents or flocks of birds. He was to note his soundings in shoal waters and enter them on a chart – with ink dots for a sandy bottom, for instance, and crosses for a rocky one. The captain was to hold regular religious services and punish blaspheming. Gambling, as a major source of discord, was, in theory, strictly forbidden and if cards or dice were found they were to be thrown overboard. If there were several ships they were to keep together and each master was given the signal code, based on showing lanterns – one or two or three displayed vertically – flying flags, firing guns or lowering sail. The code covered: land in sight, come aboard for conference, reduce sail, I am changing course, enemy sail in sight. In fog, or when huge waves or driven spray made visibility poor, contact was to be maintained by sounding trumpets and drums or, *in extremis*, for powder supplies had to be conserved, by firing guns. Sealed orders, to be opened if ships became separated, contained charted or verbally described rendezvous. Quiros' pilots, for instance, if they became separated on the long haul across the Pacific in search of Terra Australis, were to put in at Graciosa Bay on Santa Cruz Island in the Solomons, which Quiros knew from his earlier voyage with Mendaña. 'The captain who arrives first in this port, which is at the head of the bay, between a spring of water and a moderate-sized river, with bottom from 35 to 40 fathoms, is to anchor there and wait there three months for the two other ships. If by chance the other ships do not arrive, the captain, before he departs, is to raise a cross, and at the foot of it, or of the nearest tree, he is to make a sign on the trunk to be understood of him who next arrives, and to bury a jar with the mouth closed with tar, and containing a narrative of all that has happened and of his intentions.

Then he will steer s.w. as far as 20°, thence n.w. to 4°, and on that parallel he is to steer west in search of New Guinea.' Instructions varied in detail but all can be summed up in Sir John Hawkins' laconic formulation: 'Serve God daily, love one another, preserve your victuals, beware of fire, and keep good company.'

A study of the mathematically sophisticated books on navigation printed during the Renaissance, and the elaborate and beautiful astrolabes used by astrologers and astronomers for measuring the angle of stars above the horizon, gives a quite false impression of the standard of scientific navigation at sea. Pilots were seldom educated men, their solar or stellar observations were made from a tiny pitching platform, and, most important of all, there was no accurate way of telling the time. Because celestial observation depends on the time difference between the spot where an observation is made and the elevation of the sun or star at the time-point in Europe which is used as the basis of the conversion tables, it is important to be accurate, at least within a few minutes. Time was kept by the half-hour glass, turned eight times in each four-hour watch. A delay in turning it – excusable enough when all hands were coping with a squall – could throw out calculations for the rest of the voyage, and, after weeks and months away from home, the inevitable small errors in manufacture made matters cumulatively worse. In theory, it was possible to tell the time by means of a nocturnal. This was a disc with a peep-hole in the middle for looking at the pole star and a swivelling pointer to align on one of the pole star's 'guards', Kochab. A scale running round the disc showed the pointer's position for midnight on each day of the year. The pilot set it for the right date and waited till Kochab showed beyond the pointer: it was then midnight. It was, in fact, a coarse instrument, even in a dead calm, and there are few references to its use.

Without a chronometer it was impossible to calculate longitude, but latitude could be roughly computed with a simple form of astrolabe or with the quadrant, more popular at sea because it was simple and represented one quarter of the astrolabe's 360° disc. The quadrant was like half a protractor, with a plumb-line attached to its right-angle. While this dangled, the pilot lined up the sun or pole star through two peep holes, nipped the plumb-line against the scale and read off the angle. Sometimes the scale was marked with well-known places, like Cape Verde, instead of with degrees, a concession to actual practice when, in default of longitude, seamen sought the latitude of a known port or landmark and 'sailed latitudes', i.e. went east or west. It was still necessary to know the time in order to compare the angle with that at Lisbon, or Nuremburg, or wherever the ship's tables were printed, but the sun's shadow from the mast gave a crude enough estimate of noon. The quadrant was widely used, but it was seldom relied upon. Against a chorus of baffled vituperation from shore-based experts, seamen trusted to instinct, experience and the compass. They sailed, in fact, by dead reckoning, plotting the compass bearing and daily distance run on their chart.

The compass was, *par excellence*, the explorer's navigational aid. Indeed, it is not altogether unlikely that the history of Renaissance exploration would have been the same had no other instrument existed. Made of magnetized wire (refreshed from time to time with strokes from a loadstone), mounted on a cardboard disc marked with a wind rose, and pivoting on a pin, the compass was a thoroughly serviceable instrument though subject to variations near iron-bearing cliffs or towards the magnetic pole – variations which had painfully to be learned, voyage by voyage. Its efficiency can be gauged from this account of an incident from Jenkinson's crossing – the first by an Englishman – of the Caspian Sea in 1559.

'Sailing sometimes along the coast, and sometimes out of sight of land, the 13 day of May, having a contrary wind, we came to an anchor, being three leagues from the shore, and there rose a sore storm, which continued 44 hours, and our cable being of our own spinning broke, and lost our anchor, and being off a lee shore and having no boat to help us, we hoisted our sail and bare roomer [ran along] with the said shore, looking for present death, but as God provided for us, we ran into a creek full of ooze and so saved ourselves with our bark and lived in great discomfort for a time . . . When the storm was ceased, we went out of the creek again and having set the land with our compass and taken certain marks of the same during the time of the tempest whilst we rode at our anchor, we went directly to the place where we rode with our bark again, and found our anchor which we lost; whereat the Tartars much marvelled how we did it.'

Estimating distance was more subjective. The log-line came slowly into use towards the end of the sixteenth century. Until then the pilot judged the ship's speed by throwing a piece of wood overboard or, more likely, by simply spitting over the side and making a guess based on his experience of the vessel's performance. He also had to trust to experience in judging the amount of slip caused by currents on the ship's beam. To assist in calculating the forward distance covered during a period of tacks into the wind there was a traverse board. This was a wooden compass rose with eight peg holes along each bearing. Pegs were put in, course by course, each half-hour of the watch and, at the end of the watch the results were written down. The courses could then be plotted out with ruler and dividers on the chart, and the absolute distance found. There were also printed traverse tables, but their geometrical basis seems to have made pilots fight shy of them while the extremely primitive nature of some of the traverse boards that have survived suggests that they were in fairly extensive use.

To the compass should be added the lead. Soundings were always made in the proximity of land – 120 fathoms was a common depth for the first soundings – and the nature of the sea-bottom, deduced from what stuck in the recess near the tip of the lead, gave valuable indications of position on previously described routes, and were carefully recorded on new ones. These observations were patiently compiled in the pilotage books, known as rutters, which were the ancestors of our Admiralty Pilots. Here is a typical extract, from a rutter for the Caribbean. 'If you depart from S. Juan de Ullua to Havana, you must stir away north-east until you bring yourself in 25 degrees, and from thence you must stir away east for the little islands called Las Tortugas, until you have the sounding of them. And if you find white sand very small, you shall be east and west with them, and if your grounding be shelly ground and periwinkles, or small shells or scales, then shall you be north-east and south-west, and the shells and scales must be red. And if at some time you take up black sand, then are you north and south with the said Tortugas.'

The rutters also incorporated notes about the colour of the sea, the presence of weed, and the behaviour of birds. This is an extract from a set of pilotage instructions for the east coast of Africa. 'Steering this course, as soon as you see large numbers of seagulls from 8° to between 9° and 10° latitude, that you are off the islands of Arro, and you will find gulf-weed and branches of seaweed. On seeing these signs together with man-of-war birds and wind in the east, you should try to work south-westwards and approach Cape Delgado, and though there is likewise gulf-weed off this coast, it is not found together with seagulls and men-of-war birds.'

Another aid to navigation the shore-based experts could not work out for themselves was the way in which the winds moved over the ocean. The seas are divided into zones in which the winds blow favourably or adversely, or fail for months at a time. They can be an invisible barrier or supply a surge of free power. This unseen map of the wind routes had to be learned as painfully as the map of lands and seas beneath it. Between Mexico and the Philippines, for instance, vessels proceeded westwards below the thirtieth parallel, where the north-east trades blow steadily. The return wind-routes lay further north, where the less reliable westerlies reigned. But it was long before mariners, who had vainly sought favourable winds for an eastward passage from the East Indies, discovered how far north they had to go to find it. This exploration of the winds, which set down the world's trade routes until the coming of steam, was hardly less important than the exploration of new lands. And this could only be done at sea, by mariners constantly learning, recording their observations and passing them on to others. 'There is not a fowl that appeareth or sign in the air or in the sea,' noted an English merchant from Goa in 1579, 'which they have not written which have made the voyages heretofore. Wherefore, partly by their own experience, and pondering withal what space the ship was able to make with such a wind, and such direction, and partly by the experience of others, whose books and navigations they have, they guess whereabouts they be.'

'Guess'; with methods so rudimentary and achievements so colossal, we must regret the more how little we know of the men who made them.

6

The Further Study of Renaissance Exploration

This book is an introduction to a subject which is not only fascinating in itself, but can illuminate many other areas of history. I have not dealt with the consequences of exploration, for instance, economic and political, nor with colonies, nor with what can be learned about European societies from watching how their representatives behave in comparative isolation overseas. And there are other themes, beginning with exploration, which the reader might feel inclined to pursue: the institution of slavery, missionary activity, and the intellectual consequences of this opening of the world: the impact of exploration upon European literature, philosophy and science. This last chapter, then, is in the form of a critical bibliography, both to enable the reader to go more fully into the subject matter of this book, and to extend it.

Among general histories of exploration, two stand out: Boies Penrose, *Travel and discovery in the Renaissance* (Harvard U.P., O.U.P., 1952), which covers every aspect of the subject and has a long bibliography, and J. H. Parry, *The age of reconnaissance* (Weidenfeld & Nicolson, 1963; Mentor paperback, 1967) which is particularly full on the technical side, ships and navigation; it is, moreover, most helpfully illustrated. Knowledge of ship design and navigational methods will add greatly to the pleasure of seeing ship models (like those in the Royal Naval College Museum at Greenwich or in the Science Museum) and navigational instruments – and of looking at paintings which include them. *The Mariner's Mirror* is a scholarly periodical devoted to ships; R. & R. C. Anderson, *The sailing ship* (Harrap, 1926) the best non-technical introduction to ship design. On navigation E. G. R. Taylor, *The haven-finding art* (Hollis & Carter, 1956) is a good introduction to D. W. Waters, *The art of navigation in England in Elizabethan and early Stuart times* (Yale U.P., 1958), which is in turn an introduction to one of those subjects that lead naturally from exploration: the relationship between science and technology during the Renaissance. A recent attempt to show the connection between European technology and overseas expansion is C. M. Cipolla, *Guns and sails in the early phase of European expansion, 1400–1700* (Collins, 1966); it is both scholarly and written with great verve.

Original maps of this period are mostly priced beyond the reach of the student – charts are even more expensive – but most great libraries have collections which they are glad to show to a reasonably informed inquirer. By reading R. A. Skelton, *Explorers' maps* (Routledge, 1958) and G. R. Crone, *Maps and their makers* (Hutchinson, 2nd edn., 1966) the inquirer will be informed enough not to feel self-conscious, and a lavishly illustrated book – Leo Bagrow, *History of cartography*, edited by R. A. Skelton (Watts, 1964) will complete his confidence.

J. N. L. Baker, *A history of geographical discovery and exploration* (Harrap, 1937) is an essential reference book, invaluable for checking names, places and dates. The *Times Atlas* is excellent. Shorter, but also very good, is *The Oxford Atlas*. Then there is *The Times index-gazetteer of the world*; this enables any place mentioned in the literature of exploration to be easily identified.

Outstanding in the literature of the history of exploration are the many volumes of the Hakluyt Society. The Society edits the narratives of exploration (in English translation where necessary) with copious introductions, notes, maps and bibliographies. Most are easily identifiable by the explorer's name. I will only mention two here, *The tragic history of the sea, 1589–1622*, edited by C. R. Boxer (C.U.P., 1959), because through its narratives of shipwreck it gives the most graphic description of seaboard and castaway life that

I know, and *Europeans in West Africa, 1450–1560*, edited by J. W. Blake (Quaritch, 2 volumes, 1942), because its combination of narrative and explanatory commentary reveals the inadequacy of essays like my own. To pursue the later history of exploration as a whole there is still no rival to E. Heawood, *A history of geographical discovery in the 17th and 18th centuries* (C.U.P., 1912).

On Africa and the Far East up to the first voyage of Vasco da Gama there is E. Prestage, *The Portuguese pioneers* (Black, 1933, reprinted 1966). Thereafter there are two good books with unpromising titles: H. H. Hart, *Sea road to the Indies* (New York, Macmillan, 1950) and E. Sanceau, *Indies adventure* (Blackie, 1936). To get some idea of the Eastern civilizations with which the Europeans so brashly came into contact it is well worth reading *Memoirs of Zehir-ed-Din Muhammed Babur*, translated by J. Leyden and W. Erskine (O.U.P., 2 volumes, 1921): this is one of the great autobiographies of all time; *China in the sixteenth century, in the journals of Matteo Ricci, 1583–1610*, translated by L. J. Gallagher (New York, Random House, 1953); and an excellent anthology, *They came to Japan*, edited by M. Cooper (Thames & Hudson, 1965). Dent have published *Portuguese voyages, 1498–1633*, edited by C. D. Ley (Everyman series, 1947) and Penguin Books a translation of Camoens, *The Lusiads* by W. C. Atkinson (1952). A book to browse in, if not to read right through, is D. F. Lach, *Asia in the making of Europe* (Volume 1, *The century of discovery*, parts 1 and 2, U. of Chicago P., 1965). This deals with the interchange of contacts, information and ideas between Europe and Asia.

On the Americas the literature is, of course, enormous. It is worth beginning with *The Vinland sagas: the Norse discovery of America*, translated by M. Magnusson and H. Pálsson (Penguin Books, 1965) if only by way of preparation for the controversial *The 'Vinland map' and the 'Tartar relation'* by R. A. Skelton, T. E. Marston and G. D. Painter (Yale U.P., 1965), a book which sums up a great deal of recent work on pre-Columbian Atlantic discovery. On Columbus the best, because the most balanced and the most readable, is S. E. Morison, *Christopher Columbus: admiral of the ocean sea* (O.U.P., 1942). The author sailed Columbus' courses himself on the barkentine *Capitana* and the result is an admirable blend of yachtsman's lore and scholarship of the best detective variety. A Spectrum paperback, *The Americas on the eve of discovery*, edited by H. E. Driver (Prentice Hall, 1964), is a useful anthology, and Columbus' own accounts of his voyages have been reprinted from the original Hakluyt Society edition in *Four voyages to the New World*, edited by R. H. Major (New York, Corinth Books, 1961). For North America, T. J. Oleson, *Early voyages and northern approaches, 1000–1632*, (O.U.P., 1964) covers the voyages, B. G. Hoffman, *Cabot to Cartier* (U. of Toronto P., 1961) covers the period 1497–1550 in more detail and gives an account of the peoples discovered, and J. B. Brebner, *The explorers of North America, 1492–1806* (Black, 2nd edn., 1965) is a sound survey which strikes well inland. For the Caribbean, C. O. Sauer, *The early Spanish Main* (C.U.P., 1966) is iconoclastic and freshens a well-worn subject. On the exploration and settlement of Central and South America, F. A. Kirkpatrick, *The Spanish Conquistadores* (Black, 3rd edn., 1963) is the best introduction, and for Spain overseas as a whole, there is the recent book by J. H. Parry, *The Spanish seaborne empire* (Hutchinson, 1966). The establishment and operation of the extra-ordinary long-distance trade between the Philippines and Acapulco is the theme of W. L. Schurz, *The Manila galleon* (New York, Dutton, 1959). On English voyages, both to the Americas and else-where, J. A. Williamson, *The age of Drake* (Black, 5th edn., 1965) remains an important and highly congenial book, and a splendid example of a mass of facts kept alive by imagination is A. L. Rowse, *The expansion of Elizabethan England* (Macmillan, 1955). But for England the fundamental work is, of course, Richard Hakluyt's *Voyages*, published in 1599 and most readily available in eight volumes in the Everyman edition (Dent, 1907, reprinted 1962). After an atlas, Hakluyt is the first step towards accumulating a library of exploration – and, for that matter, a library of Elizabethan literature.

For the northern routes I do not know of a really good work devoted to the north-east passage, but there is much relevant material in Heawood, and Penguin Books have published L. P. Kirwan, *A history of polar exploration* (1962). For the north-west, E. S. Dodge, *Northwest by sea* (New York, O.U.P., 1961) is vivid and scholarly. The classic work on the Pacific is J. C. Beaglehole, *The exploration of the Pacific* (Black, 3rd edn., 1966), and to see how improved instruments and hygiene changed the nature of exploration after the Renaissance, the reader could not do better than read the same author's edition of *The journals of Captain Cook* (C.U.P., Volume 1, 1955, Volume 2, 1961, further volumes to follow). A useful Pacific reference book is A. Sharp, *The discovery of the Pacific Islands* (O.U.P., 1960).

These works are all in the mainstream of exploration literature. What is lacking in English is an attempt to tie in exploration with European history as a whole, so to break the rule that this is a bibliography of books available in English, I cite R. Mousnier, *Les XVI° et XVII° siècles* (Paris, Presses Universitaires de France, 1961). *Merchants and scholars: essays in the history of exploration and trade*, edited by J. Parker (O.U.P., 1966) shows what sort of work can be done to connect overseas with stay-at-home themes, and while there is no general book which explores the influence of the discoveries on the way Europeans thought, I have tried to sketch an answer in a chapter 'Geographical horizons and mental horizons' in *The age of the Renaissance*, edited by D. Hay (Thames & Hudson, 1967) and there are two books which will show how suggestive this topic is: L. Hanke, *The Spanish struggle for justice in the conquest of America* (O.U.P., 1950) and R. R. Cawley, *Unpathed waters: studies in the influence of voyages on Elizabethan literature* (O.U.P., 1940). Further material, with illustrations, will be found in my *Age of Exploration* (Time/Life, 1966). Other topics which lead from Renaissance exploration are the extension of Christianity – and K. S. Latourette, *A history of the expansion of Christianity* (New York, Harper, 7 volumes, 1937–45) is much less formidable than it looks; international rivalries, to which theme an excellent introduction is A. P. Newton, *The European nations in the West Indies, 1403–1688* (Black, 1933); and economic organization, on which see volume 4 of *The Cambridge economic history of Europe*, 'The economy of expanding Europe', edited by E. E. Rich and C. H. Wilson (C.U.P., 1967).

Finally, three round-trips: Ferdinand Magellan's *First voyage round the world* (1519–22) as described by his companion Antonio

Pigafetta, translated by Lord Stanley of Alderley, in the Hakluyt Society edition (1874); Drake's circumnavigation (1577–80) in the contemporary narrative in the Everyman edition of *Hakluyt's voyages*, volume 8; and, not an explorer but a very open-eyed Florentine merchant, Francesco Carletti, *My voyage round the world*, translated by H. Weinstock (Methuen, 1965), a voyage which lasted from 1591–1606 and is itself an enthralling tribute to the explorers who had blazed his lengthy zig-zag trail.

Books published since the first printing of this study:

J. H. Parry, *The European reconnaissance: selected documents* (N. Y., Harper Torchbooks, 1968). Imaginatively chosen extracts from accounts of voyages, travellers' impressions and navigational handbooks. Useful maps and a valuable chronological table.

J. H. Elliott, *The old world and the new, 1492–1650* (Cambridge, England, U.P., 1970). A careful assessment of the impact in Europe of the American discoveries.

Samuel Eliot Morison, *The European discovery of America,* Volume I: *The northern voyages A.D. 500–1600.* (O.U.P., 1971). The most striking account of the exploration of North America.

Appendix

Exploration: the First Hundred Years: Some Dates

Date	Africa and Far East	The Americas
1434	Cape Bojador rounded	
1473	Lopo Gonçalves crosses equator	
1485	Diogo Cão reaches Cape Cross	
1488	Bartholemew Dias rounds Cape of Good Hope	
1492		Columbus, 1st voyage
1493		Columbus, 2nd voyage
1497		John Cabot reaches Newfoundland
1498	Vasco da Gama reaches India	Columbus, 3rd voyage
1499		Probable discovery of Brazil by Vespucci
1500	Madagascar discovered	Cabral reaches Brazil
1501		Vespucci explores east coast of South America
1502		Columbus, 4th voyage
1509	Portuguese reach Malacca	Sebastian Cabot discovers Hudson Straits
1511–4	Portuguese expeditions in East Indies, Burma and Siam	
1513	Jorge Alvares visits Canton	Balboa sights Pacific
		Ponce de Leon discovers Florida
1514	Antonio Fernandes crosses Mashonaland	
1517		Spanish conquest of Mexico begins
1519–22	Magellan's circumnavigation	
1519		Alonso de Pineda finds mouth of Mississippi
1524		Verrazano explores east coast of North America
1526	Discovery of New Guinea	
1530		Spanish conquest of Peru begins
1534		Jacques Cartier, 1st voyage
1535		Cartier, 2nd voyage, reaches Montreal
		Spanish exploration of Colombia and Venezuela begins

Index

J. R. HALE, Professor of History at the University of Warwick since 1964, was formerly Fellow and Tutor of Jesus College, Oxford and is the author of a number of books and articles on Renaissance history and is a contributor to the first three volumes of the *New Cambridge Modern History*. He is at present working on *Renaissance Europe*, forthcoming in the *Fontana History of Europe* series. He developed a taste for travel, and for the literature of discovery, during the last war, when he spent three years in the Merchant Service, visiting many of the countries mentioned in this book from the West Indies to New Zealand and from Iceland to the Cape of Good Hope. This interest has been sustained by his researches into the development of Renaissance fortification, of which he is planning a comprehensive history. This work has involved investigating Spanish ports in the Caribbean, and Portuguese ones on the Zambezi, on the coast of East Africa from Sofala to Malindi, in the Persian Gulf, from Diu to Cochin on the coast of India and, farther east, at Macao. While this experience does not entitle him to any claim to be an explorer, certain regions, like some of the now uninhabited Querimba Islands, certain means of transport, like dug-out canoes and dhows, and certain feelings of isolation and uncertainty, have enhanced his admiration for the pioneers of Renaissance exploration and, he hopes, his understanding of them.